Other titles in the A Retreat With... *Series:*

Anthony of Padua: Finding Our Way, by Carol Ann Morrow

Benedict and Bernard: Seeking God Alone—Together, by Linus Mundy

Black Elk: Living in the Sacred Hoop, by Marie Therese Archambault

Brother Lawrence and the Russian Pilgrim: Praying Ceaselessly, by Kerry S. Walters

Catherine of Siena: Living in the Truth, by Elizabeth A. Dreyer

C. S. Lewis: Yielding to a Pursuing God, by Robert F. Morneau

Elizabeth Seton: Meeting Our Grace, by Judith Metz, S.C.

Francis and Clare of Assisi: Following Our Pilgrim Hearts, by Murray Bodo, O.F.M., and Susan Saint Sing

Francis de Sales, Jane de Chantal and Aelred of Rievaulx: Befriending Each Other in God, by Wendy M. Wright

Gerard Manley Hopkins and Hildegard of Bingen: Turning Pain Into Power, by Gloria Hutchinson

Jessica Powers: Loving a Passionate God, by Robert F. Morneau

Job and Julian of Norwich: Trusting That All Will Be Well, by Carol Luebering

John the Evangelist: That You May Have Life, by Raymond E. Brown

Luke: Stepping Out on the Word of God, by Barbara E. Reid, O.P.

Mark: Embracing Discipleship, by Stephen C. Doyle, O.F.M.

Mary of Magdala and Augustine: Rejoicing in Human Sexuality, by Sidney Callahan

Matthew: Going Beyond the Law, by Leslie J. Hoppe

Mother Teresa and Damien of M... Those Who Suffer, by Joan Guntzelman

Oscar Romero and Dorothy Day: Walking With the Poor,
by Marie Dennis

Our Lady of Guadalupe and Juan Diego: Heeding the Call,
by Virgilio Elizondo and Friends

Our Lady, Dominic and Ignatius: Praying With Our Bodies, by
Betsey Beckman, Nina O'Connor and J. Michael Sparough, S.J.

Patrick: Discovering God in All, by Timothy Joyce, O.S.B.

Pope John XXIII: Opening the Windows to Wisdom, by Alfred McBride,
O. Praem.

Teresa of Avila: Living by Holy Wit, by Gloria Hutchinson

Thea Bowman and Bede Abram: Leaning On the Lord,
by Joseph A. Brown, S.J.

Therese of Lisieux: Loving Our Way Into Holiness,
by Elizabeth Ruth Obbard, O.D.C.

Thomas Merton: Becoming Who We Are, by Dr. Anthony T. Padovano

A Retreat With Desert Mystics

Thirsting for the Reign of God

Linus Mundy

ST. ANTHONY MESSENGER PRESS
Cincinnati, Ohio

Scripture citations are taken from the *New Revised Standard Version Bible*, copyright ©1989 by the Division of Christian Education of the National Council of Churches of Christ in the U.S.A. Used by permission. All rights reserved.

We are grateful for permission to quote material printed by the following publishers:

Reprinted by permission of Andrews McMeel Universal, excerpts from *The Hermitage Journals: A Diary Kept While Working on the Biography of Thomas Merton*, by John Howard Griffin, copyright ©1983. Reprinted by permission of Cistercian Publications, excerpts from the *apophthegmata patrum*, the alphabetic collection, from the translation of Sister Benedicta Ward SLG, and published in *The Sayings of the Desert Fathers*, Cistercian Studies Series Number 59, copyright ©1975. Reprinted by permission of Liguori Publications, excerpts from *Listen to the Desert*, by Gregory Mayers, copyright ©1996. Reprinted by permission of the Society for Promoting Christian Knowledge, excerpts from *Asking the Fathers*, by Aelred Squire, copyright ©1973. Reprinted by permission of Abingdon Press and Darton, Longman & Todd, excerpts from *The Wilderness of God*, by Andrew Louth, copyright ©1991. Reprinted by permission of Random House, Inc., excerpts from *The Desert Fathers*, by Helen Waddell, copyright ©1998. Reprinted by permission of The Thomas Merton Center, excerpts from "Moses as Exemplar: The Paradoxes of Thomas Merton," *The Merton Seasonal*, by Patrick Reilly, copyright ©1996. Reprinted by permission of New Directions Publishing and the Trustees of the Merton Legacy Trust, excerpts from *New Seeds of Contemplation*, copyright ©1961, *The Asian Journal*, copyright ©1975 and *The Wisdom of the Desert*, copyright ©1960, by Thomas Merton. Reprinted by permission of HarperCollins San Francisco and the Trustees of the Merton Legacy Trust, excerpts from *Run to the Mountain: The Journals of Thomas Merton*, copyright ©1995, edited by Patrick Hart, OSCO, and *Entering the Silence: The Journals of Thomas Merton*, copyright ©1996, edited by Jonathan Montaldo. Reprinted by permission of Curtis Brown, Ltd. and the Trustees of the Merton Legacy Trust, excerpts from *The Seven Storey Mountain*, by Thomas Merton, copyright ©1976. Reprinted by permission of the Trustees of the Merton Legacy Trust, excerpts from *The Contemplative Vocation* (Credence Communications audiocassette), by Thomas Merton.

Cover illustration by Steve Erspamer, S.M.
Cover and book design by Mary Alfieri

ISBN 0-86716-371-2

Published by St. Anthony Messenger Press
www.AmericanCatholic.org
Printed in the U.S.A.

Dedication

To you,
Emily,
my precious

Contents

Introducing A Retreat With...

Twenty years ago I made a weekend retreat at a Franciscan house on the coast of New Hampshire. The retreat director's opening talk was as lively as a long-range weather forecast. He told us how completely God loves each one of us—without benefit of lively anecdotes or fresh insights.

As the friar rambled on, my inner critic kept up a *sotto voce* commentary: "I've heard all this before." "Wish he'd say something new that I could chew on." "That poor man really doesn't have much to say." Ever hungry for manna yet untasted, I devalued any experience of hearing the same old thing.

After a good night's sleep, I awoke feeling as peaceful as a traveler who has at last arrived safely home. I walked across the room toward the closet. On the way I passed the sink with its small framed mirror on the wall above. Something caught my eye like an unexpected presence. I turned, saw the reflection in the mirror and said aloud, "No wonder he loves me!"

This involuntary affirmation stunned me. What or whom had I seen in the mirror? When I looked again, it was "just me," an ordinary person with a lower-than-average reservoir of self-esteem. But I knew that in the initial vision I had seen God-in-me breaking through like a sudden sunrise.

At that moment I knew what it meant to be made in the divine image. I understood right down to my size eleven feet what it meant to be loved exactly as I was.

Only later did I connect this revelation with one granted to the Trappist monk-writer Thomas Merton. As he reports in *Conjectures of a Guilty Bystander*, while standing all unsuspecting on a street corner one day, he was overwhelmed by the "joy of being...a member of a race in which God Himself became incarnate.... There is no way of telling people that they are all walking around shining like the sun."

As an absentminded homemaker may leave a wedding ring on the kitchen windowsill, so I have often mislaid this precious conviction. But I have never forgotten that particular retreat. It persuaded me that the Spirit rushes in where it will. Not even a boring director or a judgmental retreatant can withstand the "violent wind" that "fills the entire house" where we dwell in expectation (see Acts 2:2).

So why deny ourselves any opportunity to come aside awhile and rest on holy ground? Why not withdraw from the daily web that keeps us muddled and wound? Wordsworth's complaint is ours as well: "The world is too much with us." There is no flu shot to protect us from infection by the skepticism of the media, the greed of commerce, the alienating influence of technology. We need retreats as the deer needs the running stream.

An Invitation

This book and its companions in the *A Retreat With...* series from St. Anthony Messenger Press are designed to meet that need. They are an invitation to choose as director some of the most powerful, appealing and wise mentors our faith tradition has to offer.

Our directors come from many countries, historical eras and schools of spirituality. At times they are teamed to sing in close harmony (for example, Francis de Sales, Jane de Chantal and Aelred of Rievaulx on spiritual friendship). Others are paired to kindle an illuminating fire from the friction of their differing views (such as Augustine of Hippo and Mary Magdalene on human sexuality). All have been chosen because, in their humanness and their holiness, they can help us grow in self-knowledge, discernment of God's will and maturity in the Spirit.

Inviting us into relationship with these saints and holy ones are inspired authors from today's world, women and men whose creative gifts open our windows to the Spirit's flow. As a motto for the authors of our series, we have borrowed the advice of Dom Frederick Dunne to the young Thomas Merton. Upon joining the Trappist monks, Merton wanted to sacrifice his writing activities lest they interfere with his contemplative vocation. Dom Frederick wisely advised, "Keep on writing books that make people love the spiritual life."

That is our motto. Our purpose is to foster (or strengthen) friendships between readers and retreat directors—friendships that feed the soul with wisdom, past and present. Like the scribe "trained for the kingdom of heaven," each author brings forth from his or her storeroom "what is new and what is old" (Matthew 13:52).

The Format

The pattern for each *A Retreat With...* remains the same; readers of one will be in familiar territory when they move on to the next. Each book is organized as a seven-session retreat that readers may adapt to their own schedules or to the needs of a group.

Day One begins with an anecdotal introduction called "Getting to Know Our Directors." Readers are given a telling glimpse of the guides with whom they will be sharing the retreat experience. A second section, "Placing Our Directors in Context," will enable retreatants to see the guides in their own historical, geographical, cultural and spiritual settings.

Having made the human link between seeker and guide, the authors go on to "Introducing Our Retreat Theme." This section clarifies how the guide(s) are especially suited to explore the theme and how the retreatant's spirituality can be nourished by it.

After an original "Opening Prayer" to breathe life into the day's reflection, the author, speaking with and through the mentor(s), will begin to spin out the theme. While focusing on the guide(s)' own words and experience, the author may also draw on Scripture, tradition, literature, art, music, psychology or contemporary events to illuminate the path.

Each day's session is followed by reflection questions designed to challenge, affirm and guide the reader in integrating the theme into daily life. A "Closing Prayer" brings the session full circle and provides a spark of inspiration for the reader to harbor until the next session.

Days Two through Six begin with "Coming Together in the Spirit" and follow a format similar to Day One. Day Seven weaves the entire retreat together, encourages a continuation of the mentoring relationship and concludes with "Deepening Your Acquaintance," an envoi to live the theme by God's grace, the director(s)' guidance and the retreatant's discernment. A closing section of Resources serves as a larder from which readers may draw enriching books, videos, cassettes and films.

We hope readers will experience at least one of those memorable "No wonder God loves me!" moments. And we hope that they will have "talked back" to the mentors, as good friends are wont to do.

A case in point: There was once a famous preacher who always drew a capacity crowd to the cathedral. Whenever he spoke, an eccentric old woman sat in the front pew directly beneath the pulpit. She took every opportunity to mumble complaints and contradictions—just loud enough for the preacher to catch the drift that he was not as wonderful as he was reputed to be. Others seated down front glowered at the woman and tried to shush her. But she went right on needling the preacher to her heart's content.

When the old woman died, the congregation was astounded at the depth and sincerity of the preacher's grief. Asked why he was so bereft, he responded, "Now who will help me to grow?"

All of our mentors in *A Retreat With...* are worthy guides. Yet none would seek retreatants who simply said, "Where you lead, I will follow. You're the expert." In truth, our directors provide only half the retreat's content. Readers themselves will generate the other half.

As general editor for the retreat series, I pray that readers will, by their questions, comments, doubts and decision-making, fertilize the seeds our mentors have planted.

And may the Spirit of God rush in to give the growth.

Gloria Hutchinson
Series Editor
Conversion of Saint Paul, 1995

Getting to Know Our Directors

Introducing the Desert Mystics

Studying the Desert Mystics makes me think of the F. Scott Fitzgerald line about how the rich are different than us: "They have more money." Let's face it: The Desert Mystics were "different" than us. They had more holiness than us—or at least that's our romantic image of them. And this is certainly not a book that attempts to bash these holy men and women, but to offer them as models for our own holiness. These are some of the people who can help us desire not to *seem* good but to *be* good.

How did these early Christians go about getting "richer" than us? What can we learn from these *truly rich* (truly holy) men and women?

This book is one in a long list of publications that attempt to bring ancient wisdom—ancient "secrets of holiness"—to contemporary culture. This book attempts to *un*cover and *dis*cover the gems of prophecy and inspiration that our Christian forebears in the desert knew.

Mystics that they were, they sought nothing less than an intimate knowledge of *God*. And that is the pearl of great price that we modern spiritual seekers continue to "lay down our money" for. And so we ask during this weeklong retreat: Who were the Desert Mystics? What did they do? Why did they do it? Should we follow them? These are the central questions that come to mind. And with the answers we can hope to modify our own lives and practices—to "be like them"—and to come ourselves to a more intimate knowledge of God.

Barring that—if we find we can't *really* go out and "be like them," perhaps we can be like them during the weeklong duration of this retreat! Do you remember the rich young man of the Gospels, the would-be follower of Jesus? Wanting to cut to the chase, the young man asks Jesus, "Teacher, what good deed must I do to have eternal life?" Jesus answers methodically, "[K]eep the commandments." The rich man says, "I have kept all these; what do I still lack?" Jesus said to him, "If you wish to be perfect, go, sell your possessions and give the money to the poor, and you will have treasure in heaven; then come, follow me." The passage sadly concludes: "When the young man heard this word, he went away grieving, for he had many possessions" (Matthew 19:16-22).

No, that's not like being a vegetarian between meals! It's more like going without a between-meal snack for a week. Maybe we can try that one. In my own life, and in the life of the Church, I see that even Lent is not a permanent season.

So within these pages you will find an introduction to the lives and practices of the fourth- and fifth-century Egyptians, most of them laypeople, who are known collectively as the Desert Fathers, the Desert Elders—or Desert Mystics, as we shall refer to them in this retreat. There were also a few women among them, and they will be highlighted, as well.

In order to draw closer to God, these spiritual pioneers went to the desert. Among them were: Saint Antony of Egypt (also often referred to as Antony), perhaps the archetypal Desert Mystic. There was also Macarius the Great, Abba Moses and many more. Each of these great seekers left the cities and trampled into the wilderness. They lived in unadorned, austere solitude—

some as hermits, some in loosely organized communities or colonies. Above all, history credits these Desert Mystics with the creation of an ascetic tradition of prayer and penance—a tradition that has flowed though the centuries like a steady river down to our own times.

And so we ask the Desert Mystics, just as Jesus asked the crowds when referring to John the Baptist (Matthew 11:7-8): "What did you go out to the desert to see? A reed swayed by the wind? Then what did you go out to see? Someone dressed in fine clothing? Those who wear fine clothing are in royal palaces." Jesus knew there was much more than reeds and royal riches out there in the drylands; there was a prophet there. "Yes, I tell you, and more than a prophet" (Matthew 11:9).

In fact, the desert was a veritable school for prophets!

Jesus tells us that to find our lives we must lose our lives. The Desert Mystics took up this radical exhortation and lived it out radically. (If you care to call that "*living*"!) What they can teach us, if we are ready for them on this seven-day retreat, is to confront our very God on a most intimate level—by confronting ourselves fiercely and fully.

Placing Our Directors in Context

The World of the Desert Mystics

"Get right with God" was a popular highway sign when I was a child. I always thought it was pretty fanatical, myself. Maybe it was just too simplistic for me. And yet...

I have always admired people who have the courage to "take things to the limit," and do it with style, with panache! For this reason I've long admired Thomas Merton who gave up everything to become a Trappist, a monk with initials after his name that proclaim, "I am a monk whose lifestyle is all about *Strict Observance*. I have come here to Get Right With God. Period." Likewise, I admire modern prophets who can shake us out of our complacency (though there are very few of them left); actors who can go "over the top" to move us to laughter or tears; singers who can hit that perfect note way up there above all the rest; poets who can write volumes in single words!

And then there are those whose very lives are or were exaggerated, "taken to the limit," for God. And while their lives and their example inspire us, we need not copy their actions or their lives entirely. Rather, we can adapt from them. Indeed, one can have a "monk soul" without living in a monastery. One can become an everyday monk or mystic without even totally standing out in a crowd!

With that, let's back up and ask—and attempt to answer—some of the most basic questions:

Who Were the Desert Mystics?

Let's say they were a "curious" sort of folk, albeit what they were most curious about was *God*. They lived and prayed in the fourth and fifth centuries; Saint Benedict—the founder of all Western monasticism—was to come later. How were they "curious"? They went into trances; they levitated; they sat on top of poles; they were often found in a state of ecstasy. *And all of this before lunch!* (And you don't want to know what they had for lunch!)

And just who were these curious God-seekers, what are their names? There is a brief introduction here to only a few of them, in order to give a sense of who they are and what they lived for. Many biographies and commentaries are listed in the back of this book for those who care to deepen their acquaintance with these holy people.

The best-known Desert Mystic was Antony—also

known as Antony the Great. We'll look into his life and practice first. He lived to be over a hundred years old, dying in the year 356. His life story, written by Athanasius, goes something like this (and I here compress a whole century into a few paragraphs):

Antony was an Egyptian, the son of well-to-do Christian parents who died when he was a teen. One day in church he heard: "If you wish to be perfect, go and sell your possessions and give the money to the poor, and…come follow me" (Matthew 19:21). He felt the words were meant specifically and literally for him. He sold everything and gave the proceeds to the poor, then went to the feet of an old man in an adjoining village who had spent his life in solitary prayer. Gradually, he withdrew, going farther and farther from home. First, it was to live in tombs, then in the desert itself, living in solitude in a deserted fort for twenty years.

As he lived there, "never going out and seldom seen," he attracted great renown, only to eventually have a mob break down his door and join him—whether he wanted them to or not! On came an ever-increasing number of seekers wanting his advice and seeking to pursue the ascetic life under his guidance. Eventually Antony withdrew even deeper into the desert, about a hundred miles from Cairo. Antony spent the rest of his life there, occasionally visiting other monks in the area and receiving people from "the world" who came to visit him.

What does this story not tell? That Antony loved his desert life! Says Athanasius, in his *Life of Saint Antony*, "At the base of the mountain there was water, crystal-clear, sweet, and very cold. Spreading out from there was flat land and a few scraggly date palms. Antony…fell in love with the place."[1]

The above story also does not tell just what a sight it was when Antony's 55-year-old face was first seen after twenty years of self-imposed exile:

> Antony came forth as out of a shrine, as one initiated into sacred mysteries and filled with the Spirit of God.... When they saw him, they were astonished to see that his body kept its former appearance, that it was neither obese from want of exercise, not emaciated from his fastings and struggles with the demons....The state of his soul was pure...all balanced, as one governed by reason and standing in his natural state.[2]

Another Desert Mystic was Abba Moses, best remembered, perhaps, for his simple yet profound saying: "Go and sit in your cell, and your cell will teach you everything."[3]

And then there was Macarius the Egyptian. Called both Macarius the Great and Macarius the Elder, Saint Macarius the Egyptian lived around 300 to 390. He was a camel-driver earlier in life and lived as an anchorite until he was falsely blamed for a local girl's pregnancy. At about age thirty, he joined a colony of monks in the desert of Scete and became widely known for his holiness and miracles. He was ordained a priest around 340. Like many of the early monks, he traveled a lot and was not fixed in any one place.

Arsenius was born in Rome about 360. A well-educated person of senatorial rank, Arsenius was appointed by the Emperor Theodosius as tutor to the princes, Arcadius and Honorius. He left the palace in 394 and secretly sailed off to Alexandria. From there he went to Scetis and put himself under the guidance of yet another Desert Father, Abba John the Dwarf. He was renowned for his silence and austerity (in stark contrast to the opulence he had experienced in Rome). He died at the mountain of Troe in 449.

Evagrius of Ponticus belonged to a community of

ascetic monks living in widely scattered individual huts on the Egyptian desert some fifty miles from Alexandria. Evagrius was one of the first monks to formulate a list of cardinal or "deadly" sins, or "destructive passions." (We will elaborate on them elsewhere during our retreat week.) He wrote particularly about *accidie*, a spiritual temptation that plagued many hermit monks who tried to live the minimal desert life after having come from the secular world of hustle and bustle and sensory stimulation. John Cassian, a fifth-century monk in Marseilles, extended and clarified Evagrius' writings and made them useful to later centuries of Christianity, including, of course, our own. It was Evagrius who described the Desert Monk's life, the life of the solitary, as "separated from all, and united with all."

What Did They Do?

They went into the desert to pray—pure, undisturbed prayer was their aim…and their daily challenge. Their secret was to make it so that, in their lives, God was unavoidable.

But that wasn't any easier then than it is now: The life of Antony and, for that matter, a great many stories and accounts of the Desert Mystics, tell us about demons. The desert was a perfect place to encounter them, perhaps even the place to seek them out and deal with them. So much of the mystic's time in the desert was spent on fighting these demons—primarily the demons whose single objective was to keep the monk from praying, to keep the monk from God.

Writer Andrew Louth tells us in his book, *The Wilderness of God*, that:

> For much of the desert tradition, two words are almost synonymous: *logismos* and *demon*. *Logismos* means a "thought," and the *logismoi* we encounter

> in the writings of the Desert Fathers are thought to be caused by demons...trains of thought, strings of considerations, that invaded the heart, occluded it, divided it, and destroyed any chance of a single-hearted devotion to, search for, God.[4]

Today we may call this particular demon by another name—such as "distractions." Every earnest prayer is all too familiar with them. And what's worse, says Louth, is that:

> Even if one manages to be quiet for a few moments, one's mind starts off on a train of thought about how spiritual one has become, how successfully one can pray! It is not difficult to imagine how greatly distraction can be magnified if one is keeping silent not just for twenty minutes but for hours at a time.[5]

Even though the notion of demons, the devil, was a much more commonplace notion back in the early centuries of Christianity, we still have many other demons today, of course, and we see the fruits of their works. In our popular culture, perhaps we call these demons things like: commercials, bearish stock markets, trade deficits, low ratings on opinion polls, computer crashes, bad hair days.

But for the spiritual seeker, there is perhaps an even more insidious—if shorter—"blacklist." Two demons that come to mind quickly are Noise and Speed. We will talk about these two demons in our retreat sessions. Both can kill; and every serious spiritual seeker combats them daily—just as the early Desert Christians did. In this way, in fact, the Desert Mystics were to become "everyday martyrs," even if they couldn't become "real" martyrs. Aelred Squire, in his book, *Asking the Fathers*, relates that Antony, for one, in his earlier life was deliberately exposing himself to the possibility of arrest and execution; it was what a good Christian did back then.

But, alas,

> His was to be the almost more exacting path of discovering how to be an authentic Christian in a less dramatic way. For, as Athanasius informs us in a telling and instructive phrase, "when the persecution finally ceased, Anthony went back to his solitary cell; *and there he was a daily martyr to his conscience*, ever fighting the battles of faith."[6]

What else did the Desert Mystics do? They became spiritual masters, teachers and sages—composers of practical wisdom based on their ascetic experiences. These teachings are best known today as the sayings of the Desert Fathers and there are various collections of them. Certain themes run throughout these collections—repentance, obedience, and the importance of stillness, the cell and prayer.

These sayings were most often short, to-the-point teachings directed at a particular "inquiring disciple." Desert Mystic Evagrius Ponticus is the first of the desert fathers whose sayings of this kind were collected in a written form.

One point that must be restated here is that these Desert Mystics were seen as, and were revered as, spiritual masters. They were steeped in the Scriptures, and many, though not all, were themselves learned students of the classical theology and philosophy of their time. (With some of the less learned among them we could say it was not *what* they knew, but *Who* they knew that mattered.) Their teachings always extended the Biblical texts, applying them to the individual and his/her circumstances. But more than all this, the Desert Mystics lived the Scriptures—and it was evident for all to see and hear.

It is most interesting what we do *not* find in the sayings: Gregory Mayers writes in *Listen to the Desert*:

> ...[W]hen we turn to the direct accounts of the life of the desert gathered by the monks themselves, we encounter something altogether strange and foreign. These writings are collections of brief, loosely connected passages that range in length from a few sentences to a page or two. The stories and sayings were gathered by the monks, who circulated these writings among themselves for their own purposes. In these collections...we find little direct record of artfully arranged accounts of the sort of life that the monks led. We find no programs for spiritual advancement, no body of doctrine, no specific rules of conduct. When first turning to these writings the reader might be disappointed, for there is little that stimulates the intellect and imagination, inspires the spirit, or edifies the soul. The sayings of the old men give us a glimpse into a hard life, lived close to the desert floor in heat and cold. These stories and sayings were no doubt quite instructive to the ancients who shared that life and to those who have striven to emulate it since, but they can seem more than a little eccentric by modern standards.[7]

As to their cells or living spaces, we find a variety of possibilities existed, a common one being monks living in separate cells grouped together at a distance from one another, the monks coming together to celebrate Eucharist. The cell itself was intentionally simple, even dull, so that distractions would subside and the monk could concentrate on doing what he came into the desert to do: to pray.

Historians believe that the daily cycle of monastic prayer, now commonly known as the Hours or the Divine Office, got its start here in the desert traditions (in the Palestinian pattern and practice if not in the Egyptian) as the Desert Mystics ordered their prayer lives after a set discipline.

Here, too, the Jesus Prayer got its start ("Lord, Jesus, Son of God, have mercy on me, a sinner"; these Mystics knew that the desert was a place for repentance) as well as the repeated recitation of the psalter, the Psalms, which the monks were expected to have memorized. The Psalms, of course, are the heart and soul of the monk's daily prayer, and have been through the ages.

Why Did They Do It?

Well, one might go so far as to say they did it because it was the "easiest" way—or, at least, the surest way, to holiness. Thomas Merton, at the beginning of another hard Lent almost six years after entering the austere life of the Trappist monk, wrote:

> The greatest joy in life is to give up yourself altogether for the honor and glory of God, to know you belong to him entirely, that your will is owned, possessed by His love. Anything that tends to that end, any sacrifice, therefore, brings joy and happiness, even though it may be bitter to the flesh. However, there is nothing especially bitter about our fast. I am glad to be able to take at least what our present Rule offers.[8]

Merton added the next day, "If it is this way when we do penance, what is it going to be like in heaven?"[9]

But why did they really go through all that trouble and sacrifice to become Desert Mystics? Because they believed this particular thing was what God wanted them to do. It was the right thing to do. To them, the quest for God meant "ascetical withdrawal" from the world—the renunciation of society, marriage, family, property, the ordinary comforts and pleasures and ambitions most humans experience.

In order to put the Desert Mystics into proper historical context, just the briefest bit of early Church history is in order here. The most concise history I have found, and the one I like the most because it puts this "Call of the Desert" era into such fine overall perspective, is C. H. Lawrence's *Medieval Monasticism*. I will attempt to summarize its "Call of the Desert" chapter as a way of putting our retreat directors, the Desert Mystics, into the larger historical context.

First of all, it is important to remember that in the first centuries of the Church there was a great deal of persecution of Christians going on, and the possibility of becoming a martyr for Christ was a very good one. So far so good: any devout and fervent Christian worth his or her salt at the time was more than happy to die for the faith, and huge numbers did. (It is said that Antony of the Desert, even after the persecution centuries, hoped to become a martyr, but it didn't come to pass; so he shed sweat instead of blood.) The point being made here is this: After Christianity became legal, and even imperially recognized, it appears that for many it may have gotten too "easy." So, to oversimplify all this: This is a big part of the reason the desert call was so clear and inviting—here was a chance to live the more authentic life that Christ was talking about in the Gospels, to really take up some crosses.

The deserts to which the early ascetics were called were in Egypt, Syria and Palestine. And there were essentially two ways of life they chose: the life of the hermit (eremitic) or life in a community monastery (cenobitic; the first such organized community was established by Saint Pachomius [c. 292-346]). The colonies of hermits contained several hundred solitaries living in caves or huts, generally out of earshot of each other. In the center of the settlement were such entities as a bakery, a church to gather in for Eucharist, a space for pious guests and sightseers. The hermits made their living by making baskets, ropes, mats and linens, which they exchanged with people in the villages for their basic necessities.

"Fasting, deprivation of sleep, and other forms of bodily mortification, were the standard weapons of the ascetic's armoury in the struggle for self-conquest," says C. H. Lawrence in *Medieval Monasticism*.[10] Lawrence goes on to relate some of the more exotic and extraordinary stories many of us have heard about these curious folks. One of these was about Macarius (d. 393). Macarius had heard of the superhuman practices of the monks of Saint Pachomius—and he vowed to top them!

> As Lent came on, Macarius observed that some of the brethren fasted for two days together, and one of them for a whole week, while others spent half the night standing in prayer. So he made his dispositions to outdo them all. He took up his stand in a corner and remained there praying and plaiting mats, without food, drink, or sleep, until Easter.[11]

This sort of extravagant practice, this "competitive asceticism," was quite common, we find. Some of the most bizarre stories come out of Syria, where, for example, Saint Simeon the Stylite took up residence on top of a pillar, where he remained, exposed to the sun and weather for forty-seven years! This was his dramatic way of withdrawing from the world.

Some real pioneering was also going on in the desert, as we have said above. It was in the newly established communities—"loose communities" that they were—that the earliest monastic traditions of a common meal, obedience to a superior, the daily round of collective worship, the importance of prayer and work, were taking place. Here is where monastery life as we still know it today was "abirthing."

Why a monastic *community*? (After all, the word *monastery* is derived from the word *mono*, meaning "alone" or "single".) It was Saint Basil of Caesarea, himself a hermit for a time, who left a lasting mark on monastic tradition by concluding that, yes, the hermit who seeks freedom in the desert to be alone with the Alone was indeed fulfilling the first great commandment. But what about the second? "The defect of the solitary life was that it provided no opportunity to practice the virtues of humility and patience or to perform practical works of mercy—'If you live alone, whose feet will you wash'?"[12]

What Can We Learn From Their Lives, Their Sayings, Their Teachings?

No one could describe better just how "accessible" or "digestible" the lives, the teachings, the sayings of the Desert Mystics are to us moderns. Here are the "appetizing" words of Bob Walker, in his introduction to the book, *Listen to the Desert*:

> ...[A]s we take up these stories, one by one, it is possible to discover that, driven more by appetite than by hunger, we have grown used to going to our kitchens absent-mindedly, expecting to find a loaf of bread. By opening these writings, we feel as if we have come to a cupboard where we are now faced with only a bag of flour, a box of salt, and a package of yeast, and we have no sure ideas about how to transform these into something that will feed our growing hunger. But herein lies the peculiar power of these writings to place us face to face with these old monks. It is the time we spend with the ingredients—the mixing, the rising, the baking, the buttering—it is the time we spend before we sink our teeth past the warm crust, that places us in closer context with the ancient world and allows the

> strangeness of that world to shape itself, gain texture, and grow increasingly familiar.[13]

But what can we learn from these ascetics? For one thing: We learn that it's OK (and even necessary) to experiment, to some degree, in the spiritual life. Indeed, almost every type of monastic life was tried, shaped, and reshaped among the Desert Mystics.

Secondly, we learn caution. We can learn a lot from a Desert Mystic—without literally "becoming" one. There is always the danger that we try to "put on" what doesn't fit us. As Thomas Merton wrote:

> Saint Gregory said that there are men who try to be contemplatives when it is not their vocation. You can tell by the way everything about their life becomes complicated and upset. They do not find peace, but only turmoil in trying to live an entirely inward life. For them the thing to do is to pluck out the eye of contemplation that scandalizes them and enter into eternal life with one eye, i.e., action. From that you can conclude that the normal thing is to have both eyes, contemplation and action. *Per se* everyone is called to both, *per accidens* it is better to give up one or the other to *some extent*.[14]

Do you remember the first time you discovered Saint Francis of Assisi—and you wanted to be just like him? Well, even Francis made it clear he wasn't trying to get everyone to be like him. He wanted us to "do" the Christian life in the way *God* chose for each of us.

But, as Merton put it, we can conclude that the normal thing is to have "both eyes" to look at all of this: Namely, we can never *be* Christ, but we must always try to be *like* Christ. That's the message to take home during this week of retreat. The Desert Mystics took things further beyond the limit most of us would set. But their ultimate motive, their ultimate goal of loving God, is one that we, too, freely and completely claim for ourselves.

Finally, we can learn a lot from them by studying their sayings. The sayings of the Desert Fathers can provide much food for inspiration and meditation. As stated above, these sayings are collections of stories, anecdotes, maxims, proverbs—all of which assumed written form after many years of belonging only to the oral tradition. The Reflections throughout this book offer some samples of these powerful sayings. In *The Wilderness of God*, Andrew Louth writes of these sayings,

> They are not intended to be read systematically, rather their pithy, gnomic form are intended to provide many different points of contact with the very varied experience of humankind. Some sayings will strike home to one person, some to another; some will seem directed to my condition now, some will only become relevant later on.[15]

Let's close with just one example: "When you see a young man ascending up to heaven through his own will, seize him by the foot and pull him down, for this is good for him."[16]

Notes

[1] Andrew Louth, *The Wilderness of God* (Nashville, Tenn.: Abingdon, 1991), p. 56.

[2] Louth, p. 56.

[3] Gregory Mayers, *Listen to the Desert* (Liguori, Mo.: Triumph Books, 1996), p. 1.

[4] Louth, p. 60.

[5] Louth, p. 60.

[6] Aelred Squire, *Asking the Fathers* (New York: Morehouse-Barlow, 1973), p. 112.

[7] Mayers, p. xxi.

[8] Jonathan Montaldo, editor, *Entering the Silence: The Journals of*

Thomas Merton (San Francisco, Cal.: HarperCollins, 1996), p. 168.

[9] Montaldo, p. 169.

[10] C. H. Lawrence, *Medieval Monasticism* (London: Longman, 1984), p. 6.

[11] Lawrence, p. 7.

[12] Lawrence, p. 10.

[13] Mayers, p. xxii.

[14] Montaldo, p. 182.

[15] Louth, p. 64.

[16] Benedictina Ward, *The Wisdom of the Desert Fathers* (Spencer, Mass.: Cistercian Publications, 1997), p. 34.

Day One

Embracing Spiritual Dryness—*Entering In as the Way Through*

Introducing Our Retreat Theme

> *"Avoid all places where you do not hear the word 'eternity' mentioned frequently."*[1]

This was the advice of Charlie Rich, a man who lived a life of quiet prayer and has been the subject of a number of books and the article, "A Life Like Few Others." This is surely the best advice of the Desert Mystics—to us. They, too, lived a life like few others. They marched to the beat of a different drum, mostly because they felt they had to. For them, it was either march to a different drum, or don't march.

By "marching," I am referring to making progress in the spiritual life, of course, and by that I mean getting alone with God, paying attention to God, living a life in love with God and God's will, giving glory to God.

The Desert Mystics show us that "spiritual dryness" is a common experience for all who seek God, and that willingly entering into this dryness is the only way to the "Oasis." As Thomas Merton puts it in his *New Seeds of Contemplation*:

> We do not go into the desert to escape people but to learn how to find them; we do not leave them in order to have nothing to do with them, but to find

out the way to do them the most good. But this is only a secondary end. The one end that includes all others is the love of God...However, the truest solitude is not something outside you...; it is an abyss opening up in the center of your own soul. And this abyss of interior solitude is a hunger that will never be satisfied with any created thing.[2]

Opening Prayer

Dear God,
Is the hard way really the easiest?
Am I putting more energy into running
  away from you
Than from just giving up and submitting
  to your will?
Isn't it time to quit this chase and
Let you catch me?
May I hear with new ears your words to me
From the prophet Hosea:
"I will now allure her;
and bring her into the wilderness
And speak tenderly to her;
I will take you for my wife forever:
I will take you for my wife in right and
  in justice,
In steadfast love and in mercy;
I will take you for my wife in faithfulness;
And you shall know the Lord."
  (Hosea 2:14, 19-20)
Amen.

Retreat Session One

Let's begin our retreat about the desert experience by looking not at the desert but at its very opposite, water, and by examining some of the sayings of the Desert Mystics as a way of elaborating on today's theme of Spiritual Dryness.

First: A Drink of Water

Why? Because so often in the spiritual life we find that we come to knowing by the way of not knowing; we come to know God by coming to know all too well that which is *not* God!

Water is life. And no one knows this better than those who live in arid lands. Ask a farmer who is trying to be positive about his crops during a long drought. Ask a person on dialysis whose water intake is strictly limited.[3] As you think of water, what images come to mind? Do you think of its healing qualities? Or water as the quencher of thirst? Or its cleansing qualities? Let's take one of these at a time:

Water heals. Jesus in the Gospels uses water and the image of water repeatedly. He tells one lame person to go wash in the water; he heals a blind man by applying spit to the eyes and then telling the man to wash in the waters of Siloam.

Water quenches. Contrary to what TV commercials try to tell us, the drink we really want when we are thirsty is water. Our bodies are made up of water more than anything else, and this water must be replenished daily or we become dehydrated.

Water cleanses. Jesus went so far as to say in John's Gospel: "Until I wash you, you have no share with me"(John 13:8b).

In a church in southern California there is a stream of water running down the center of the aisle connecting the baptistery and the altar. During moments of silence, worshippers can hear the sound of gentle gurgling and splashing from the running water, as if to remind the congregation of the journey of faith which begins in Baptism and leads to our final home: the throne of God. What a fine and subtle reminder of the life of a Christian!

In the desert it was less subtle, of course. When water flows in the desert, one dances for joy! When one comes upon an oasis, one comes upon nothing less than *life* itself!

Desert Sayings and Stories

Here are two stories of the hardships—and aridity—of the desert life. But, more than that, these are stories of faith, and trust and Providence. As we read this saying, let us be thinking about today's theme—spiritual dryness—and how this is a theme as pertinent to today's spiritual seeker as it was to one in the early Christian centuries:

> One day Macarius the Egyptian went from Scetis to the mountain of Nitria for the offering of Abba Pambo. The old men said to him, "Father, say a word to the brethren." He said, "I have not yet become a monk myself, but I have seen monks. One day when I was sitting in my cell, my thoughts were troubling me, suggesting that I should go to the desert and see what I could see there. I remained for five years, fighting against this thought, saying, perhaps it comes from the demons. But since the thought persisted, I left for the desert. There I found a sheet of water and an island in the midst, and the animals of the desert came to drink there. In the midst of these animals I saw two naked men, and

> my body trembled, for I believed they were spirits. Seeing me shaking, they said to me, "Do not be afraid, for we are men." Then I said to them, "Where do you come from and how did you come to this desert?" They said, "We came from a monastery and having agreed together, we came here forty years ago. One of us is an Egyptian and the other a Libyan." They questioned me and asked me, "How is the world? Is the water rising in due time? Is the world enjoying prosperity?" I replied it was and then I asked them, "How can I become a monk?" They said to me, "If you do not give up all that is in the world, you cannot become a monk." I said to them, "But I am weak, and I cannot do as you do." So they said to me, "If you cannot become like us, sit in your cell and weep for your sins." I asked them, "When the winter comes are you not frozen? And when the heat comes do not your bodies burn?" They said, "It is God who has made this way of life for us. We do not freeze in winter, and the summer does us no harm." That is why I said that I have not yet become a monk, but I have seen monks.[4]

How many of us think (know!) that we, too, are weak, and "cannot do as you do." I am reminded of that wonderful line in the movie *Raiders of the Lost Ark*, where Indiana Jones and one of his helpers have finally found the chamber in the desert where the Ark of the Covenant has been buried. Looking down into the ominous chamber from above, Indy's helper sees the floor beneath them covered with crawling snakes. He turns to Indy and says, "Very dangerous; *you go first!*"

Well, the Desert Mystics went first! They "go before us." And Jesus went before them. All of our ancient Christian heroes not only went before us to show us the way, but have also gone before us in experiencing hardship, desperation, spiritual dryness. But they came through with shining colors, in the end—just as Indiana Jones always does—because they embraced the dryness. "I hate snakes!" Indy repeats a number of times throughout the movie. They are his greatest nemesis—and they're everywhere, of course!

What do *we* hate the most as we travel our journey toward holiness and God? Perhaps it is the dullness of our deserts that dries up our energies. For the Desert Mystics, life was intended to be pretty dull in order to let distractions subside. The monk's major occupations were all, in themselves, the ultimate in dullness: working at some simple, undistracting labor such as basketmaking, both eating and sleeping sparingly. So it is that Abba Poeman states:

> Living in your cell clearly means manual work, eating only once a day, silence, meditation; but really making progress in the cell means to experience contempt for yourself wherever you go, not to neglect the hours of prayer and to pray secretly. If you happen to have time without manual work, take up prayer and do it without disquiet.[5]

There is a long list of "hardship" Desert sayings to examine for inspiration as we face our own brand of "spiritual dryness." One worth close study is the story of a desert elder visited by "an angel of the Lord" who convinced him of the ultimate good inherent in a measured dose of hardship, sacrifice and dryness:

> A certain old man dwelt in the desert, and his cell was far from water, about seven miles and once when he was going to draw water, he flagged and said to himself, "What need is there for me to endure this toil? I shall come and live near the water." And saying this, he turned about and saw one following him and counting his footprints: and he questioned him, saying, "Who art thou?" And he

> said, "I am the angel of the Lord, and I am sent to count thy footprints and give thee thy reward." And when he heard him, the old man's heart was stout, and himself more ready, and he set his cell still farther from that water.[6]

As with every good story there is, of course, comfort and consolation in the end—and the river of God flows even through the center of the desert:

> It was said of Abba Macarius the Egyptian that one day when he was going up from Scetis with a load of baskets, he sat down, overcome with weariness and began to say to himself, "My God, you know very well that I cannot go any farther," and immediately he found himself at the river.[7]

For Reflection

- *Do you ever believe that "the hard way is really the easiest"? When have you taken the hard way to holiness—on purpose? Francis of Assisi, Mother Teresa and Dorothy Day lovingly took "the road less traveled" as the way to God. In what way might these choices have made their lives "easy"?*
- *Jesus, the font of life who quenched the world's great thirst for God, died crying: "I thirst." Meditate for a few moments on the magnitude of God's great gesture to quench our thirst.*
- *For which quality of the water of life do you most desperately thirst? For what do you need healing? Cleansing? In what way do you thirst for a deeper relationship with God?*

Closing Prayer

Like the deer that yearns for running streams,
So my soul is yearning for you, my God.
My soul is thirsting for God, the God of my life;
When can I enter and see the face of God?
My tears have become my bread, by night, by day,
As I hear it said all day long: "Where is your God?"
Deep is calling on deep, in the roar of waters;
Your torrents and all your waves swept over me
(adapted from Psalm 41).

Notes

[1] "A Life Like Few Others," by John W. Donohue, S.J., *America*, 9/28/96, p. 22.

[2] Thomas Merton, *New Seeds of Contemplation* (New York: New Directions, 1962), p. 80.

[3] Thanks to S. M. Terence Knapp, O.S.B., for her generous sharing of this material with the author. The text is modified from a Scripture reflection she presented to the author's faith community.

[4] Ward, *The Sayings of the Desert Fathers*, pp. 125-126.

[5] Louth, p. 65.

[6] *The Desert Fathers*, Helen Waddell (New York: Random House, 1998), p. 94.

[7] Ward, p. 130.

Day Two

Voluntary, Extravagant Exile—*Turning the World's Standards Upside-Down*

Coming Together in the Spirit

What would you think of the idea of gathering up all of your possessions, stacking them in a big pile (yes, the computer and the big-screen TV and the microwave and that great novel you're reading)...and then just walking away? Or: What would you think about taking all your ideas, your plans, your brilliant Microsoft Word documents, putting them all onto a single hard drive or master diskette, and then hitting the "Delete" button?

Well, this is pretty much what the Desert Mystics did. And they did it without looking back (very much). The secret? While they knew just what they were walking away from, and while they knew just what they were deleting, they knew even better what they were walking *toward*...and what they were intending to *create* of themselves there in the desert.

Defining Our Thematic Context

The Desert Mystics knew the Gospels; they were familiar with them and studied them feverishly. And so it was that Jesus' exhortation in Luke (17:33) that "Those who try to make their life secure will lose it, but those who lose their life will keep it" did not fall on deaf ears. Nor did the passage Jesus spoke about riches and renunciation go unnoticed or unheeded: "Truly, I tell you, there is no one who has left house or wife or brothers or parents or children for the sake of the kingdom of God, who will not get back very much more in this age and in the age to come eternal life" (Luke 18:29-30).

More basically still, they knew and lived the gospel command to "Take up your cross and follow me."

When a monk goes to a monastery, the monk is really entering a desert—a deserted place. And there are plenty of crosses there in the desert. As I write this, I am in the midst of a deserted place that is filled with crosses everywhere you look. It's the Abbey of Gethsemani and I am here on retreat, praying with the Trappists here. And a desert it is—a truly deserted place in the middle of a deserted countryside. The symbols here are not accidental: One passes through the center of a cemetery to get inside this desert; one promptly sees the big stone letters spelling "God Alone" on the stone wall. And the message is clear: "Abandon everything *but* hope—all ye who enter here."

Thomas Merton said of this place: "This is the center of America." And two paragraphs later: "This is the only real city in America—in a desert." He was referring to Gethsemani, of course. But more than that he was referring to the deserts we can choose to go to. "Gethsemani [read: your desert place] holds this country together the way the underlying substrata of faith that goes with our own being and cannot be separated from it, keeps living a man who is faithless..."[1]

Monks—all holy people and all who seek holiness in the desert of their lives—may well be accused of being "useless." After all, what do they really *do*? One answer, besides Merton's answer of "holding this country together," is inspiring the good and holy in others, much the way art inspires us. And what is art? It is a work or creation that has an exaggerated, dramatic, extraordinary element to it. It has an "edge" to it that the amateur may not even be able to identify. I recall Mozart, after one of his marvelous concerto creations, writing to his father, saying something like: "I've done it, Dad! I've created something that everyone will like. Some will even know *why* they like it; others will just like it and not be sure just why!"

I like being here in a desert called Gethsemani, and I'm not absolutely certain just why! I'm in a monastery retreat-house desert with: no phone, no mail, no fax, no voice mail or E-mail or even snail mail; no meetings, no meals to cook, no dog to feed, no lawn to mow, no interruptions except the ones I choose. Everything is simple here.

But the thing to remember (and one notices quickly!) is that there is also: no morning newspaper, no Starbucks coffee, no La-Z-Boy rocker, no Budweiser, no NBA basketball, no baby's smile, no record-breaking sales reports, no letter from friend Dave, no homemade rhubarb pie, no wife and kids and dog who love me.

"Spectacular view. Wide-open spaces. No cable." That's a headline in a recruitment ad I saw recently. It's the same recruitment headline modern spiritual seekers are responding to.

Opening Prayer

Lord, help me to empty myself,
Rather than fill myself,
So that there might be room enough
for you.
Amen.

Retreat Session Two

Ultimately, the Desert Mystics went looking for God's will. They did it by giving up, renouncing and carving away everything that was not God. It's much like the story of the old woodcarver who was asked how he could make such a wonderful sculpture of a mule out of a block of wood: "I just carve away everything that ain't mule."

And they came to know "by the way of unknowing." It is always this way in the spiritual life, the way of paradox and surprise. We put "Ann's Birthday" on our calendar when we should be putting "Show Ann you love her" there; we think we want to live to "contemplate" when what God wants us to do is to live to love...others, self, God. In our lives in general it is the same: Writer Annie Dillard, who in my mind is nothing less than a modern mystic, says:

> We are making hay when we should be making whoopee; we are raising tomatoes when we should be raising Cain, or Lazarus...I won't have it. The world is wilder than that in all directions, more dangerous and bitter, more extravagant and bright.[2]

The Desert Mystics remind us to boil all of this thing called life down to its bare essentials, its very essence. It is only love that matters; it is only love that lasts. In the

Gospels we hear again and again where folks tried to get it out of him: Jesus, what would *you* do? What *is* the answer? Is it true that "all we need is love"? That's *it*?! "Oh, yes," says Jesus, "and that means loving the utterly undesirable ones also. As a matter of fact, especially them! You are to seek them out; you're to go out of your way to find them and hold them and love them. In fact, I command you not only be in favor of people hugging lepers; *you* are to hug them yourself!"

When we come to the desert we leave behind our self-importance, our money, our fitness-club membership cards and our home shopping network account number. We turn in our CD's, our BMW's, our IBM's, our PIN's, our URL's and our VIP status. Here each of us is just a vip, all in lower case. There's no dot com, either!

And there is very little Speed, very little Noise. These are two modern "demons" we referred to earlier, but which are worth a bit more study in any examination of desert spirituality.

Do you know how slowly life moves (or doesn't move!) in the desert? As a Midwesterner, I do not know it firsthand, but have read much about the desert and have traveled America's west and southwest enough to be struck by the deafening stillness. One can quickly say how this desert environment could inspire such a desert saying as: "Say nothing unless it will improve upon the silence."

The desert folks called it *quies*, quiet. Thomas Merton wrote of it as *silentio: "Bonum est praestolari cum silentio salutare Dei."* ("It is good to wait in silence for the salvation of God.")[3]

I was recently reading an article in *National Geographic* about an expedition to the Antarctic Desert. One of the most striking comments one explorer made was something near to: "The Desert: At first you think there's nothing there, don't you? *And then there is too much.*" Wow. I think it's the same with the fourth-century desert the early Mystics walked through...not to mention the one *we* are journeying through!

Let's close with two Desert Stories—two quotations from the sayings, each recorded, no doubt, for their dramatic power:

> It was said of him that he had a hollow in his chest channeled out by the tears that fell from his eyes all his life while he sat at his manual work. When Abba Poemen learned that he was dead, he said weeping, "Truly you are blessed, Abba Arsenius, for you wept for yourself in this world! He who does not weep for himself here below will weep eternally hereafter; so it is impossible not to weep, either voluntarily or when compelled through suffering."[4]

> The brethren also asked him [Agathon], "Amongst all good works, which is the virtue which requires the greatest effort?" He answered, "Forgive me, but I think there is no labour greater than that of prayer to God. For every time a man wants to pray, his enemies, the demons, want to prevent him, for they know that it is only by turning him from prayer that they can hinder his journey. Whatever good work a man undertakes, if he perseveres in it, he will attain rest. But prayer is warfare to the last breath."[5]

And, finally, an instructive story to reinforce our understanding of today's retreat theme of Turning the World's Standards Upside-Down. This is an especially meaningful story for those of us who feel we have some sort of "inside track":

> Some elders once came to Abbot Anthony, and there was with them also Abbot Joseph. Wishing to test them, Abbot Anthony brought the conversation around to the Holy Scriptures. And he began from

the youngest to ask them the meaning of this or that text. Each one replied as best he could, but Abbot Anthony said to them: "You have not got it yet." After them all he asked Abbot Joseph: "What about you? What do you say this text means?" Abbot Joseph replied: "I know not!" Then Abbot Anthony said: "Truly Abbot Joseph alone has found the way, for he replies that he knows not."[6]

For Reflection

- *From* The Wisdom of the Desert Fathers: *"A monk who was given to hard work saw someone who was carrying a dead man on a bier and he said to him, 'Do you carry the dead? Go and carry the living.'"*[7] *When have your spiritual practices been "backwards" or incomplete?*
- *"To whom much is given much is expected." What do you think God really expects of you? Is any part of that just what you expect of you?*
- *If monks are "useless," Desert Mystics are surely totally useless—except for the fact that they might be saving the world! Thomas Merton said as much when he first came to the monastery of Gethsemani. To paraphrase him: Except for the prayers of these people, the world would have blown itself apart by now. How does your prayer make a difference in the world?*
- *Have you ever noticed in a bed of flowers that the dried-up bloom, the formerly most beautiful part of a plant, is what is given up for seed? When have you given up the beautiful parts of yourself to bloom for God?*

Closing Prayer

Send rain to my roots, O God of all Creation,
That I may grow straight and tall
In your loving Presence.
For it is only you who can make the desert bloom.
May I flower in the desert, Lord,
For you.
Amen.

Notes

[1] Patrick Hart, O.C.S.O., editor, *Run to the Mountain: The Journals of Thomas Merton* (San Francisco, Cal.: HarperCollins, 1995), p. 333.

[2] Annie Dillard, *Pilgrim at Tinker Creek* (New York: Harper and Row, 1974), p. 268.

[3] Thomas Merton, *New Seeds of Contemplation* (New York: New Directions, 1962), p. 46.

[4] Ward, *The Sayings of the Desert Fathers*, p. 18.

[5] Ward, pp. 21-22.

[6] Thomas Merton, *The Wisdom of the Desert* (New York: New Directions, 1960), p. 52.

[7] Ward, p. 55

Day Three

Seeking Deeper Certitude— *Meeting God and Self Fully and Fiercely*

Coming Together in the Spirit

On this retreat day we have a "laundry list" of concepts to discuss and meditate on. And as we look at the laundry list, you will see that, indeed, we will be taking ourselves to the cleaners! And there we will have the opportunity to renew our baptismal vows and be washed clean again by the waters of God, the water present even in the driest desert!

Here are the topics we will explore in this session: (1) We are all on a journey; life is a continuum; (2) We are asked by God to keep "raising the stakes," to keep growing spiritually to a higher and higher plane; (3) It is in the desert that the Holy Spirit calls us in order to ever increase our faith and practice, our self-understanding and our God-understanding; and (4) We go there together and seek ever greater ways to serve the Lord.

Defining Our Thematic Context

Fourth-century writer John Cassian says that it is only in intensity, in "heating up" our spiritual lives, that true good can come. How do we get our spiritual lives "heated up"? One way is to go to the desert wasteland—a place where the only things that survive the heat are the things that can thrive in the heat!

This is what the Desert Mystics did. They intentionally let God turn up the heat in their spiritual lives, forcing themselves to make a fundamental choice: Do I keep feeding this fire, or let it burn out? Christ says we are to keep feeding it.

We'll use the following Desert Saying to help set the scene:

> Abba Lot went to see Abba Joseph and said to him: Abba, as much as I am able I practice a small rule, a little fasting, some prayer and meditation, and remain quiet and as much as possible I keep my thoughts clean. What else should I do? Then the old man stood up and stretched his hands toward heaven, and his fingers became like ten torches of flame and he said to him: If you wish, you can become all flame.[1]

Opening Prayer

Holy Spirit,
Light the fire of your love within me.
Help me to understand that it is only in
Letting my own desires be consumed
That I become free to serve you and your will.
May the Desert Mystics
Inspire in me an intense devotion
To be more and more like Jesus,
Who reigns with you and the Father.
Amen.

Retreat Session Three

Have you ever been desperate to act? Have you ever been in a burning building and the choice was either to act quickly, desperately—or die? Have you ever had your back totally up against the wall, and the next move had to be yours or you were going to be annihilated? In this chapter we are going to talk about being desperate. Because it is out of desperation, crisis, conflict that positive action comes.

The truth is that we, too, can achieve the level of holiness of the desert mystics. Unfortunately, though, we may have to be desperate before we believe that. In many lives it takes a great personal crisis, loss or tragedy to get us to set our priorities straight. Sometimes we need to lose it all, everything, before we can begin to gain anything.

Usually the type of loss we are talking about is an involuntary loss: a loved one dies, we get a dread disease, we lose a job, someone we love is suffering and we feel helpless. We experience a crisis in faith—faith in our world, our God, our selves.

In the case of the Desert Mystics of history, they seemed—insanely enough—to invite God to help *create* such a crisis point or loss! (I always tell people to stop beating themselves up—there are plenty of other people who will gladly do that for you!) Why, then, would anyone *invite* a crisis? *To see if they can pass the test.*

The desert is a school, then—a place to learn, to discover. And to be tested.

What Do We Learn?

What are the wild discoveries? We learn humility and purity of heart—we hear and respond to God's invitation to be like him, work like him, witness like him, pray like him, sweat like him, suffer like him, die like him. After all, desert spirituality is Gospel spirituality if it is anything.

It is in the desert that so many of the classic Gospel texts start hitting home:

> If any want to become my followers, let them deny themselves, take up their cross, and follow me. (Matthew 16:24)

> No one can serve two masters; for a slave will either hate the one and love the other, or be devoted to the one and despise the other. You cannot serve God and wealth. (Matthew 6:24)

> If you wish to be perfect, go, sell your possessions and give the money to the poor, and you will have treasure in heaven; then come, follow me. (Matthew 19:21)

> Those who find their life will lose it, and those who lose their life for my sake will find it. (Matthew 10:39)

And, finally, the one Scripture citation that I think more than any other may have inspired so many of these folks to leave their homes and go into self-exile:

> Beware of practicing your piety before others in order to be seen by them; for then you have no reward from your Father in heaven...your Father who sees in secret will reward you. (Matthew 6:1, 4)

In the desert one is not on display—except perhaps to the varmints who seek to destroy you! But our piety and devotion are private and personal, and only God knows what we're doing there.

What else do we learn in the desert? Intensity! God knows that while we're there learning a lot about God, we are also learning a lot about our very selves and some of it is not so pleasant, perhaps. In my own life, spending time in the wide-open wasteland of my soul, I readily come to see what's wrong with: my wife, my kids, my boss, my pastor, my job and my God—it's *me*!

We learn about meeting God and ourselves fully and fiercely. That means we make commitments; we say yes to the dance. We don't "sorta" dance; it's not even possible. We don't "sorta" play in God's playground; you can't "sorta" play—every kid knows that. We don't "sorta" pray; you give yourself without holding back.

We learn the blissful, hypnotic value of some great "S" words: Simplicity, Silence, Solitude, Serenity, Seclusion, Solemnity, Sacred, YeSSSSS...!

What do we say YeSSSSS to? To God, of course. And the answer must be this Yes to tougher and tougher questions as times goes on. Consolation and spiritual complacency are not to be ours. If we are getting too comfortable in our spiritual lives, we are not growing. We need not only let God build a fire, we need to keep adding fuel to it. Only when the fire is hot enough and dangerous enough do we see the very reason for the fire: It is to keep us sweating; it keeps us running to God as a man with his hair on fire runs toward water!

Flannery O'Connor's short story, "A Good Man Is Hard to Find," tells the story of a person who needed this kind of intensity just to be "good." It was only when an escaped murderer held a gun to the person's head did she become "better." Says O'Connor's Misfit character after shooting the old woman: "She would have been a good woman if it had been somebody there to shoot her every minute of her life."[2]

Do we, too, need that kind of intensity to be "good"? Well, most of us certainly need to keep close to the fireplace to stay warm; we need to keep the eternal flame burning—close by, and right there in front of us. When we do this we discover—wonder of wonders!—that like the burning bush of Moses it is a fire that rages and yet does not destroy what it burns.

We also learn there is yet another reason to go to the heat of the desert wasteland: The desert is a *refugium peccatorum*—a "refuge of sinners." Where else can you go when you're so unworthy? In one of his recorded talks to his Trappist novices in the 1960's entitled "The Contemplative Vocation," (Credence Cassettes), Merton asks the novices, "Just why did you come to this desert?" What he, the teacher, wanted his students to reply, was, "Because this is what Jesus told me to do; it's right there in the Gospels [see Matthew quotations above]." While waiting on a novice's reply, he half-humorously mutters beneath his breath, "Well, I know why I came here: It's a *refugium peccatorum*!"[3]

In other words, Merton saw the desert as a place to run to in order to do some penance for his past sins. He wanted to leave the comfort zone and go into the danger zone—a place where he could make up for past weaknesses and grow stronger at the same time.

When he did come to this refuge of sinners, he not only had the opportunity to "pay" for his sins and enter "rehab," as it were; he quickly came to the realization that this was a desert place in which to venture ever deeper and deeper. It became, in fact, a sweat lodge of sorts: a place to be locked away and be put under a heat lamp until the truth comes out. The desert is, indeed, a place of discernment, a place to sweat and ponder and figure things out. Merton knew, in fact, that the searing desert was the place you ended up—if you did it God's way.

Listen to the powerful desert imagery Merton uses in the conclusion to his classic *The Seven Storey Mountain*. He closes his book with the following words he hears God saying to him:

> I will lead you into solitude. I will lead you by the way that you cannot possibly understand, because I want it to be the quickest way...Everything that can be desired will sear you, and brand you with a cautery....You will be praised and it will be like burning at the stake. You will be loved, and it will murder your heart and drive you into the desert... But you shall taste the true solitude of my anguish and my poverty and I shall lead you into the high places of my joy and you shall die in Me and find all things in My mercy which has created you for this end and brought you from Prades to Bermuda to Saint Antonin to Oakham to London to Cambridge to Rome to New York to Columbia to Corpus Christi to Saint Bonaventure to the Cistercian Abbey of the poor men who labor in Gethsemani: That you may become the brother of God and learn to know the Christ of the burnt men.[4]

It is this same circuitous, change-centered, intense journey that must be ours. And what must always be the end result of figuring things out for us "ordinary" Christians? *Conversion*. Conversion, in fact, is the first and primary vow a Trappist/Benedictine takes when joining the religious order. He or she takes a vow, promising God and sisters and brothers to always be converting, changing, always beginning again. "Always we begin again" is the popular Benedictine motto. It was John Henry Newman who kept emphasizing in his writings and preachings that to change is essential; but to change often is to become perfect. Yes, the intensity and the heat will burn us, but it is a heat that forges us and sets us afire with God's love rather than desiccates and destroys.

We Learn Humility. If you begin with the premise that humility is the ground for all spiritual growth and life, as many great religious thinkers believe, you begin to understand the Desert Mystics. Bear in mind: Humility does not denigrate; it deals with the facts, and not less than the facts. It doesn't ask a kind soul to declare its unkindness. It asks the kind soul only to declare that its kindness comes from Mother or Teacher, or...Kindness Itself.

I dearly love the following desert story about loving-kindness:

> Two old men had lived together for many years and had never fought with one another. The first said to the other, "Let us also have a fight like other men do." The other replied, "I do not know how to fight." The first said to him, "Look, I will put a brick between us, and I will say it is mine, and you say, 'No, it is mine,' and so the fight will begin." So they put a brick between them and the first said, "This brick is mine," and the other said, "No, it is mine," and the first responded, "If it is yours, take it and go"—so they gave it up without being able to find an occasion for argument.[5]

Thomas Merton "translated" this kindness and desert humility this way—in one of my favorite Merton quotes, and one I keep tacked on my office wall:

> When humility delivers a man from attachment to his own works and his own reputation, he discovers that perfect joy is possible only when we have completely forgotten ourselves. And it is only when we pay no more attention to our own deeds and our own reputation and our own excellence that we are at last completely free to serve God in perfection for His own sake alone.[6]

We Learn What to Eat, and That We Are What We Eat. Abba Moses, in the first of John Cassian's Conferences, tells us it is important just which food our heart is being habitually fed:

> The movement of the heart may not unsuitably be compared to a mill worked by waterpower. It can never stop working as long as the flow of water drives it round. But the man in charge can decide whether he would rather grind wheat or barley or darnel. It will undoubtedly grind whatever the man who is working it puts into it. Just so, the mind cannot be free of the trouble of thoughts when it is being driven on by the events of life and the streams of trials that pour in upon it. But which thoughts it should admit or provide for itself, must be its own attention and care to arrange. If, as we have said, we always return to our reflections on Holy Scripture and go back to the memory of spiritual things, the desire for what is perfect and the hope of future happiness, it will be inevitable that this will give rise to spiritual thoughts which will keep our mind occupied with what we have been thinking. According to the word of the Lord, wherever the treasure of our occupations and interest lies, there too our heart will necessarily remain.[7]

We Learn to Pray. And, finally, there is one more reason to "go to the desert"—and it is perhaps the simplest and most basic reason of all: to pray. We go out to pray for the reign of God.

How did the Desert Mystics pray? Much of their prayer, interestingly, was memorized prayer. Remember, we're talking about the days long before the printing press. Thus the mystics memorized long, long texts of Scripture by heart—especially the Psalms. And one of the major advantages of having this big "catalog" of memorized texts inside their heads, was that they were able to quickly make "associations." Example: A Desert Mystic might be reciting a psalm of praise when a snake comes to pay a nighttime visit to the monk's tent. Quickly the monk's mental card catalog can refer him to Psalm 90, all about "Thou shall not fear the terror of the night..." After all, we are what we eat and we are also what we think. The thoughts and prayers and ideas we have consciously and conscientiously absorbed and captured are also the thoughts and ideas and prayers that are going to surface automatically—and, we hope, just when we need them!

And What's This About a Test? We all know about the Gospel account of Jesus going out into the desert "to be tested." Here it is according to Luke, 4:1-13:

> Jesus, full of the holy Spirit, returned from the Jordan and was led by the Spirit into the wilderness, where for forty days he was tempted by the devil. He ate nothing at all during those days, and when they were over, he was famished. The devil said to him, "If you are the Son of God, command this stone to become a loaf of bread." Jesus answered him, "It is written, 'One does not live by bread alone.'"
>
> Then the devil led him up and showed him in an instant all the kingdoms of the world. And the devil said to him, "To you I will give their glory and all this authority; for it has been given over to me, and I give it to anyone I please. If you, then, will worship me, it will all be yours." Jesus answered him, "It is written:
>
> 'Worship the Lord, your God,
> and serve only him.'"

> Then the devil led him to Jerusalem, and placed him on the pinnacle of the temple, saying, "If you are the Son of God, throw yourself down from here..." Jesus answered him, "It is said, 'Do not put the Lord your God to the test.'" When the devil had finished every test, he departed from him until an opportune time.

So...the devil's test, the desert test, is about knuckling under. The test is a lot about one's willingness to bear suffering. (Anyone in any desert knows that! The temptations are heightened there, under the duress. Where else would it even occur to anyone to want a rock to become a loaf of bread?) While the devil's temptation of Jesus is about selling out to the devil, our temptation in our desert is most often about ego: Whom do we trust? God? Or ourselves?

One of the best reasons for us to go to the desert in the first place is to get ourselves out of our own hands and to put ourselves into God's hands. If we're living on our terms, we make ourselves—not God—the boss. It's always a good exercise to look back and compare how we've done when we've been at the helm and when we let God take the helm. We can see the necessity of becoming totally dependent on God. As a matter of fact, the whole Christian life is about nothing other than affirming and reaffirming that God is in charge. The central question is: Can we stay faithful to God, even though we don't know where we're going or what's next in our lives? Can it be enough for us to believe that God knows and is in charge of all this? Are we enough at peace with God that we don't even need to know or care what's going to happen next?

These are some of the reasons we go to the desert, some of the things we learn there, some of the things that will happen there if we let them. We don't stay in the desert because we like it there, however. We stay there because God has lured us out there! God has put us there, and we have responded to God's call. We certainly don't need to understand.

For Reflection

- *Each of us carries a "desert" within, within the shanty of our hearts. You don't need to have an exotic desert location; your "heart-room," your bedroom, your back room—anywhere you can get alone with God will do. Go to your desert and get with God.*
- *Thomas Merton, in his* Asian Journal, *reminds us that: "The contemplative life must provide an area, a space of liberty, of silence, in which possibilities are allowed to surface and new choices—beyond routine choice—become manifest. It should create a new experience of time...one's own time, but not dominated by one's own ego and its demands."*[8] *What new choices do you want to make for God?*

Closing Prayer

We close with a prayer that the Desert Mystics prayed repeatedly—a Psalm that assuredly gave them the comfort of God's shade in the intense heat of the desert sun:

I lift up my eyes to the hills—
  from where will my help come?
My help comes from the Lord,
  who made heaven and earth.

He will not let your foot be moved;
he who keeps you will not slumber.
He who keeps Israel will neither slumber nor sleep.

The Lord is your keeper;
the Lord is your shade at your right hand.
The sun shall not strike you by day,
nor the moon by night.

The Lord will keep you from all evil
he will keep your life.
The Lord will keep your going out and your coming in
from this time on and forevermore. (Psalm 120)

Notes

[1] Mayers, *Listen to the Desert*, p. 54.

[2] Flannery O'Connor, *A Good Man Is Hard to Find* (Garden City, N.Y.: Doubleday-Image, 1970), p. 29.

[3] *The Contemplative Vocation*, by Thomas Merton, Credence Cassettes, 1985.

[4] Thomas Merton, *The Seven Storey Mountain* (New York: Harcourt, Brace and Company, 1948), pp. 422-423.

[5] Ward, *The Wisdom of the Desert Fathers*, p. 60.

[6] Merton, *New Seeds of Contemplation*, p. 58.

[7] Squire, *Asking the Fathers*, p. 124.

[8] Thomas Merton, *The Asian Journal* (New York: New Directions, 1969), p. 167.

DAY FOUR

Being Wary of Mirages—*Avoiding the 'Occupational Hazards' of a Spiritual Seeker*

Coming Together in the Spirit

Belden Lane, author of *The Solace of Fierce Landscapes: Exploring Desert and Mountain Spirituality*, is an expert on desert spirituality and "the desert experience." In a recent interview he summed up all that he has learned: "I don't want to presume to speak too much for the desert because it takes back everything you say about it."[1]

I couldn't agree more. The Desert Mystics are full of mystery—and paradox. And yet, in this very way they are perfectly synonymous with all of Christian life! As soon as we think we have God and ourselves figured out, we get a surprise that turns everything upside-down. The Spirit works as it will. And our best response can only be to work on acceptance of that Will.

Defining Our Thematic Context

Today we are going to talk about some of the "occupational hazards" of spiritual seekers. Of course, to the Desert Mystics these were known not as "occupational hazards," but as "demons."

What comes to mind quickly as a "demon" for anyone who might be inclined to the contemplative life? It's the danger in thinking that the desert experience is an individual one—one that gives me my own private hotline to God. Yes, each of us needs to work on our personal relationships with God; yes, God loves each and every one of us with a very personal, one-to-one love, but...but...even the desert experience needs to be a communal experience! It is a life together that the desert demands of us.

In the sixties some called it "dropping out." And while the desert does let us get away from it all, it quickly teaches us, as we go there and study and pray over the Gospels, that we can't truly be or do alone. Indeed, while the solitude of the desert can bring us silence and peace, it just as often gives us clarity of vision and tells us much about meaningful relationships and the real value of community. On a deeper level still, it teaches us about justice within community.

Speaking of justice and community, then, we must quickly address the demon that can so often come with that: the demon that has you saying to yourself, "I am working for justice. I am a person making a difference." The desert teaches us to be content with nothingness—no payback, no feeding of the ego. The desert teaches us that we are to do things for and with others simply because they are the right thing to do, and for no other reason at all. (Indeed, some purists will say that what the desert really tells seekers is nothing at all, not unlike the Zen master who replies "Do nothing" to the would-be activist who asks, "What do I do?") In fact, the emptiness of the desert teaches us that when we get right down to it, we can't and don't really do much at all; God does it! But, all the while, God does it somehow with and through us as we humbly go about our daily work and prayer.

Opening Prayer

Lord, today we pray only that we may
Remain faithful to you.
That's all.
Help us to seek you and your will alone.
And help us recognize the many false gods
Society puts up in front of us—
The gods we ourselves too often worship.
May you, Lord,
Only you,
Be glorified in all things.
Amen.

RETREAT SESSION FOUR

In this session I would like to talk more about a modern Desert Mystic, Thomas Merton. It was Merton who penned the simple line on Good Friday, 1942, his first Holy Week as a monk: "Give up everything for God." And then a few empty lines of space, followed by the lines to himself: "You say that, and you don't know what you mean."[2] One could say that his desert experience was "adolescing." But it was already genuine.

I want to continue the discussion of Merton's desert experience with the words of Professor Patrick Reilly, taken from a lecture he delivered at the University of Glasgow in 1995:

> I want to end in the desert, the desert where Merton did not so much try to find God as allow God to find him. Merton may have entered the desert in the spirit of the Desert Mystics, renouncing both world and self as illusions, intent on creating the void so

> that the spirit of God might completely fill the vacuum. But, once there, he discovered the true self and the real world, God's creations both, from which he had so long been divorced. And if world and self are not, as in Eastern mysticism, pure illusion, but are a creation of God, then it is the human task to return them to the Creator in their pristine purity. It is the last of the paradoxes of Thomas Merton: We must first annihilate all creatures, the self included, so that God may be everything and the world nothing; but only as the necessary prelude for seeking a greater solidarity with all creatures so that the world may acknowledge its Creator. You must first, as Thomas Merton, take a vow of silence in order to become a spokesman for God. You must throw away your life so that you may save it, you must abandon the world that you may possess it completely.[3]

What do we all like about Thomas Merton? He was a spiritual seeker—and a realist! He says he went to the desert (the monastery) not expecting to find God there so much as to find time and space to lament the fact that God wasn't of more prominence in his life! In "the world" we are so busy and overrun by everything we can spend our entire lives without much realizing that there is another world. This is what the Desert Mystics realized—and acted upon.

The other thing we all like about Thomas Merton was that he was a *perpetual* seeker; he was forever, ceaselessly, unendingly, *searching*. The search just never seemed to end, and we can all relate to that, no matter how blessed we are. With Merton, as we see in reading his journals, his search in many ways only began once he chose to become a Catholic Christian. First, he wanted to become a Franciscan, only to enter the Trappist Abbey of Gethsemani instead. Soon enough his Gethsemani "honeymoon" was over, as he was puzzling over becoming a Carthusian instead, or perhaps being sent off to a new Trappist foundation in Utah. Then it was the Camaldolese that tempted him; then the idea of a simple hermitage, in which he did live for three years; but then as this became too busy with visitors and distractions, he puzzled long and hard over the possibility of something even more remote: perhaps a faraway hermitage in Alaska...or New Mexico...or California...or in Asia? Farther and farther into the desert he wandered. And, of course, it was never to be alone at all, but to find and be with God alone.

Just one excerpt from his journal dated October 12, 1947—approximately six years after his entry into the Trappist monastery—gives a good flavor of dozens and dozens of later entries where he ponders and wrings his hands over God's will for his life:

> What is the use of all my lamentations about not being a contemplative if I don't take advantage of all the opportunities I get for prayer? I suppose I take the opportunities but in the wrong way. How much time do I waste looking for something to *read* about contemplation instead of shutting up and emptying my mind and leaving the inner door open to God to enter from the inside, the outer door being barred and all the blinds down?
>
> Maybe it's not the Carthusians: their cells are too fancy. And LaGrande Chartreuse with all those chapels and forty square kilometers of roofs! I feel too much like a big shot at Gethsemani: what would it be in such a palace? That is not for me. A little Charterhouse would be different. La Vendana—is that the name of one? If I want to be a Carthusian, it is to be one the way St. Bruno was, except I'd probably die in a week.
>
> I don't care: God is guiding me. He wants me in

> solitude, in poverty and alone with Him. Every time the smoke clears, the first thing I am conscious of is the Holy Ghost saying, "No, this way! Be quiet! Get off in a corner and forget things and set your house at rest and wait."[4]

This was written not a long time apart from his famous autobiography, *The Seven Storey Mountain*. Among its many references to life in the desert is the following:

> "I had come, like the Jews, through the Red Sea of Baptism. I was entering into a desert—a terribly easy and convenient desert, with all the trials tempered to my weakness—where I would have a chance to give God great glory by simply trusting and obeying Him, and walking in the way that was not according to my own nature and my own judgment. And it would lead me to a land I could not imagine or understand. It would be a land that was not like the land of Egypt from which I had come out: the land of human nature blinded and fettered by perversity and sin. It would be a land in which the work of a man's hands and man's ingenuity counted for little or nothing: but where God would direct all things, and where I would be expected to act so much and so closely under His guidance that it would be as if He thought with my mind, as if He willed with my will.
>
> It was to this that I was called. It was for this that I had been created. It was for this Christ had died on the cross, and for this that I was now baptized, and had within me the living Christ, melting me into Himself in the fires of His love.[5]

The Desert as a Means—Not an End

Another temptation of the spiritual seeker is to "fall in love" with means instead of ends. The best way to explain this is to relay to you the words of one God-seeker who says that he used to put "Prayer" on his calendar; now he just puts the word "God" there. The point, of course, is that the desert is not a destination in itself but a route to a destination. Prayer is not a destination in itself but a route—to God. In addition to the Desert Mystics, a wonderful exemplar for us "desert sojourners" is Moses.

Moses didn't go to the desert just to escape the cruel bondage of Pharaoh; rather he went there to lead his people to something far better than "escape"—to lead them on a journey that was to culminate—eventually—in the Promised Land, the land of milk and honey. (A *New Yorker* cartoon depicts Moses with his staff, leading the people, with one of the disgruntled followers saying: "We've been wandering in the desert for forty years. But he's a man—would he ever ask directions?") Indeed, the desert wasteland and desolation were to become all too familiar to Moses and the Israelites, as it must necessarily be with all Christian seekers then and now. Even Christ himself needed to pass through the harshest of deserts before entering into glory.

"There is no other way out for the holy person:" to paraphrase wandering American writer Jack Kerouac, "the holy person must sweat for God."

And the desert is the ultimate sweat lodge, no doubt. But, obviously, there are other connotations for the word, *desert*—and many of them less than pejorative. One of the connotations is that of a refuge, a sanctuary, a sacred wilderness. In our own country it is interesting to note how the early pioneers and settlers saw the wilderness only as a place to tame. It was, after all, a deep and dark place full of demons and beasts. But, as America's forests and wild lands have become few and far between, the remaining swatches of wilderness are nothing less than a refreshing refuge.

With this semi-romantic view in mind, one can readily see the danger of the modern would-be desert mystic who, when he or she has "arrived," wishes to "set up a tent for Moses and Elijah and oneself"—rather than continue on with what may sometimes seem like an unending journey.

Benedictine writer and lecturer Joan Chittister, O.S.B., is seen by many as a modern prophet. She shares much prophetic wisdom in a special section of *National Catholic Reporter*, entitled, "Millennial Wisdom Stirs in the Desert." Chittister talks about the "flight from the world syndrome" that tempts us today—and tempted seekers of old who went to the desert to escape the spiritual aridity of the cities in order to concentrate on God. She says that in order to be a monastic in a world bent on materialism, conversion is fundamental. "But conversion to what? To deserts? Hardly."[6]

With the coming of the Rule of Saint Benedict, and the formation of monastic communities, the answer became clearer, says Chittister. "Conversion was not geographical. We do not leave where we are in order to become a contemplative, otherwise the Jesus who walked the dusty roads of Galilee surrounded by lepers and children and sick people and disciples and crowds of the curious and the committed was no contemplative, was not engrafted into the mind of God."[7]

Thus it is that time and again we see nothing less than Christ-like expressions of love in the daily lives of the Desert Mystics. This love is seen time and again—not only as shown to the venerable ancients who lived among them, but to newcomers and a host of visitors. Writes Trappist Basil Pennington in his Preface to *The Desert Fathers*: "I think if I had to fasten on one single virtue to ascribe primarily to these women and men, it would be the virtue of compassion."[8] Pennington goes on to quote from the author of the "History of the Monks of Egypt" who expressed this beautifully:

> But of their humanity, their courtesy, their loving-kindness, what am I to say, when each man of them would have brought us into his own cell, not only to fulfill the due of hospitality, bit still more out of humbleness, wherein they are indeed masters, and from gentleness and its kindred qualities which are learned among them with diverse grace but one and the same doctrine, as if they had come apart from the world for this same end. Nowhere have I seen love so in flower, nowhere so quick compassion, or hospitality so eager.[9]

For Reflection

- *Read here what Thomas Merton wrote in May of 1947 (page 70 of* Entering the Silence*) and reflect on your own thoughts and beliefs about the "very good cross" you are presently bearing: "I have found myself a very good cross. Question: Just because a cross is a cross, is it the one God wants for you? Just because a thing is a nuisance, is it therefore the best thing for you? Is it an act of virtue to sit down and let yourself be snowed under by activities that threaten to ruin your contemplative life? I am called to be a contemplative. But I am not living like a contemplative... Ergo, what am I doing in the room over there? Piling up fuel for my Purgatory? Just because it is obedience, does that make it all meritorious? Pleasing to God? I wonder. I don't ask these questions in a spirit of rebellion. I would really like to know."*[10]
- *Then consider this very "real" summation from Thomas Merton's journal just a few weeks later (Oct. 19, 1947): "Anyway I am pretty sure I could never lead the life the*

first Camaldolese led, fasting four or five times a week on bread and water and reciting two psalters a day besides their Office, and going barefoot all winter in the Appenines."[11] *In what ways is God calling you to a contemplative life? When do you fast, keep silence, pray?*

- *When Christians pray, it is they (plural) praying: Give us this day our daily bread; forgive us our trespasses; Pray for us sinners... One of the dangers of running off to the desert or wilderness by oneself is that one may leave brothers and sisters behind, even spiritually. But even the desert hermits came together to Eucharist and prayer on weekends. How does community make your prayer, your faith, stronger?*

Closing Prayer

Lord, we know that the desert is not a destination,
Only a route.
And so we pray with the Psalmist:
O give thanks to the Lord, for he is good,
For his love endures forever.
Through the desert his people he led,
For his love endures forever
(Adapted from Psalm 135).
Amen.

Notes

[1] "When Grief Drove Him to the Desert, Lane Heard the Sound of Silence," by Jeanette Batz, *National Catholic Reporter*, Oct. 16, 1998, p. 15.

[2] Montaldo, *Entering the Silence*, p. 11.

[3] In *The Merton Seasonal*, Fall, 1998, "Moses as an Exemplar: The Paradoxes of Thomas Merton" by Patrick Reilly, p. 17.

[4] Montaldo, p. 124.

[5] Merton, *The Seven Storey Mountain*, pp. 226-227.

[6] "Millennial Wisdom Stirs in the Desert," by Joan Chittister, O.S.B., *National Catholic Reporter*, Feb. 19, 1999, p. 36.

[7] Chittister, p. 36.

[8] Helen Waddell, *The Desert Fathers* (New York: Random House, 1998), p. xviii.

[9] Waddell, p. xviii.

[10] Montaldo, p. 70.

[11] Montaldo, p. 126.

Day Five

Eyes on the Prize—*Focusing on Eternity, and God as 'All in All'*

Coming Together in the Spirit

I once had a dream about God. I must have been in heaven. There I was in this huge throng of people, billions and billions of us, hovering around an "open-air business meeting" that God was conducting. There God was, very busy, conferring with his "staff" of VIP's: people like Saint Peter, Archangel Michael, Mother Teresa, Mary, John the Baptist, David, Abraham and a bunch of others—all of them the "top brass." And God was very busy indeed with them, all very proper and orderly, making important decisions about this and that. But...what happened very distinctly and clearly in the midst of all this business was that God would every few moments glance out into the crowd and wave or wink at someone and then return to the busy discussions going on. Finally, and there it was, God was looking at me, giving a wink and a smile, as if to say, "Well, hello! I know you. It's good to see you again. We've talked often. Wish I had a little more time now, but maybe after this meeting we'll have a chance to get together for a while." And the most striking thing of all? God was doing this to each and every one of the eight or ten billion people out there in the crowd!

Defining Our Thematic Context

"Give up everything for God." [long space here] "You say that, and you don't know what you mean." These are words written by a modern desert monk and mystic, Thomas Merton, in a Good Friday journal entry dated April 3, 1942.[1] And then, just a day later he writes: "A contemplative is not one who lives for contemplation, but one who lives for *God alone*."[2]

At this juncture in our retreat with the Desert Mystics, we're going to look at God—and we're going to look at God looking at us! How, we may ask, can we find God—in a desert? And, secondly, how can God find us—in a desert? We have a Teacher—and some teachers—to help us with these profound questions!

What does the Teacher (God) teach our teachers (the Desert Mystics)? *More* than we can ever learn—and perhaps, to keep things in proper perspective, *less*:

> Abba Anthony was baffled as he meditated upon the depths of God's judgements, and prayed thus: "Lord, how is it that some die young and others grow old and infirm? Why are there some poor and some wealthy? And why are the rich unrighteous and grind the faces of the righteous poor?" And a voice came to him: "Anthony, look to yourself: these are the judgements of God, and it is not good for you to know them."[3]

Opening Prayer

L-I-S-T-E-N...

S-I-L-E-N-T...

E-N-L-I-S-T...

Amen.

Retreat Session Five

I once heard of a monastery described as "a training grounds for death." A bit grim, but one could say all of the Christian life is a training grounds for death—at least the death of the self. In this context, one can readily see how the Desert Mystics were "ahead of their time." Their very lives were to grow into Benedict's Holy Rule, with clear emphasis on "always keeping death before your eyes." Another way to look at this is to heed the advice of Saint Meinrad's Benedictine Archabbot Lambert Reilly, who preaches that, "We don't build our house on a bridge. And that's really where we're living now—on a bridge."

It has been said that part of the reason a more radical response to Christ's call was more common in days gone by is that people simply didn't live as long in former days. They thus had to start thinking about their "day of reckoning" much earlier. People of former generations saw a lot of disease and death all around them, frequently witnessing their own children or spouses die before their eyes. Thus one could cynically say that in former days committing oneself to lifelong prayer was not only less of a commitment than it might be today; it also seemed more urgent!

Today it is said that we are a death-denying people, and for good reason: The average person among us lives for many decades, some of us not witnessing a death of a loved one for an entire generation.

Thus when we read such spiritual advice as, "Always keep death before your eyes," we may not know what that means until we are middle-aged.

Which leads us to a fundamental question: How can we best learn about God and eternity and life and death and what is truly important in life? Answer: We find the best teachers. Indeed, Christianity has always respected the value of the master-disciple relationship. And the entire monastic tradition in Christianity is built upon the "guru-disciple" models we find in the Desert Mystics. While we all know that from a Christian perspective, there is only one Teacher, and that is Jesus, we may in the Desert Mystics find an entire "faculty" of wise instructors of faith. As we have seen elsewhere in this book, and will see more of later in this book, the Desert Mystics were consummate teachers, and they taught not only by being touchingly human models of faith, compassion and humility, *but through wonderful Zen-like stories* and "lessons."

A sampling of these "lessons" seems to be in order. And just a listing of the various themes or "Courses" treated in the Desert sayings is greatly illuminating in itself:

- That One Ought to Live Soberly
- That One Should Show Hospitality and Mercy With Cheerfulness
- Of Obedience
- That Nothing Ought to Be Done for Show
- That a Monk Ought Not to Possess Anything
- Of Self-Restraint
- Of Compunction
- That One Ought to Pray Without Ceasing
- Of Humility
- Of the Excellent Way of Life of Divers[e] Holy Men
- Of Mortification

But just how could these "recluses," so detached from the real world, bring such great gifts, such wisdom, to "the world"? What credibility—what credentials—did they have? Writer Andrew Louth answers this convincingly in his book, *The Wilderness of God:*

> Men and women visited the fathers of the desert to "seek a word." "Father, give me a word": that is the phrase we often come across. The seeking of a word, and the giving of a word...had nothing magical about it...The fathers of the desert, who lived close to Christ and in their struggles had participated in his victory, experienced this common humanity in Christ, and often knew the problems and anxieties of those who sought them out in a way that seems like clairvoyance. In some stories, their insight picks out a problem that the one seeking them was unaware of himself. Such a source of wisdom and insight, which could only be drawn on by those humble enough to seek it, was a precious gift from the desert to the world. As the French poet Edmond Jabes has said, "the desert lends to the least gesture, to the most insignificant word, a slow rhythm of beyond-silence, beyond-life." It was a wisdom characterized by a gentle common sense, and a profound trust in God.[4]

"A gentle common sense." A wonderful phrase. But it was a gentle common sense these teachers possessed because it came to them from the teachers and the Teacher *they* "studied under." In the *Life of Antony* it is emphasized that Antony, too, first sought the wisdom and experience of older and earlier ascetics before he himself ventured into the deeper solitude of the desert. And so the tradition of "Master-Disciple" or "Spiritual Fatherhood" is a long-established one. Clearly in the Desert Mystics we see a rich and diverse array of "Dear Abba" (!) material. Again and again we read phrases such as "A brother asked an

old man"; "Once they asked..."; "A certain philosopher asked..."

In short, their wisdom was *sought out*. And the wisdom they *gave out* was rooted in the Gospels. Thanks to the fact that their bits of wisdom have been recorded, and then eventually collected together, we today can so richly benefit. Remember, these teachers seldom emerged from their cells, but rather were visited by seekers of all stripes, by monks within their own monasteries and by others from farther afield. As to the monk-seekers, it was one of them, Dorotheus, who tellingly reports that "The Fathers say that to sit in one's cell is half, to visit the old men [the Elders/Monks/Mystics] is the other half."[5]

Were all of these Desert Mystics wise mentors, standing ready to pass out wisdom right and left to all who called upon them? I like Thomas Merton's statement about this in one of his journals: "...the Desert Fathers talked not about monastic spirituality but about purity of heart and obedience and solitude, and about God. And the wiser of them talked very little about anything."[6]

One wonderful Zen-like story goes like this. It is handed down to us in Andrew Louth's book, *The Wilderness of God*. It speaks "Of Obedience," in a time when obedience to one's spiritual teacher was paramount:

> For instance, there is the story told of John the Dwarf. His abba (Amoe) took a piece of wood and told him to water it. He had to go so far to fetch the water that he left in the evening and only returned the next morning. After three years the wood came to life and bore fruit. Abba Amoe took some of the fruit and carried it to the church, saying to the brothers, "Take and eat of the fruit of obedience." But the point of obedience was the submission of one's will, so that that will could become totally

> open to God. Obedience implied humility and trust, and these are the foundation of the desert life.[7]

Many other stories and sayings get even closer to the heart of our faith, centering directly on the "All in All," the God we seek. Here is a sampling, to keep us on target:

> Abbess Syncletica of holy memory said: There is labour and great struggle for the impious who are converted to God, but after that comes inexpressible joy. A man who wants to light a fire first is plagued by smoke, and the smoke drives him to tears, yet finally he gets the fire he wants. So also it is written: Our God is a consuming fire. Hence we ought to light the divine fire in ourselves with labour and with tears.[8]

And then there is this very simple yet profound saying:

> An old man said, "Just as no one can cause harm to someone who is close to the king, no more can Satan do anything to us if our souls are close to God, for truly he said, 'Draw near to me, and I shall be near to you.' But since we often exalt ourselves, the enemy has no difficulty in drawing our poor souls into shameful passions."[9]

And, finally, this most powerful story that sums up this retreat session well, I think—all about keeping our eyes on the prize, putting first things first:

> An old man was asked, "How can I find God?" He said, "In fasting, in watching, in labours, in devotion, and, above all, in discernment. I tell you, many have injured their bodies with discernment and have gone away from us having achieved nothing. Our mouths smell bad through fasting, we know the Scriptures by heart, we recite all the Psalms of David, but we have not that which God seeks: charity and humility."[10]

For Reflection

- *To paraphrase Thomas Merton: "This is my life, and I don't pretend to understand it." What are the "big" questions in your life? Where do you seek answers?*
- *Reflect for a few moments on this piece of wisdom from Meister Eckhart: "Blessed are the pure in heart who leave everything to God now as they did before they ever existed."*

Closing Prayer

Lord, I know that sometimes
You leave in us some defects of character—
So that we can learn humility.
For without these defects,
We would immediately soar above the clouds
In our own estimation—
And would place our throne there instead of yours.
Protect us, Lord, from such perdition.

—*Paraphrase of prayer of Theophane the Recluse, Desert Monk and Mystic*

Notes

[1] Montaldo, *Entering the Silence*, p. 10.

[2] Montaldo, p. 44.

[3] Squire, *Asking the Fathers*, p. 11.

[4] Louth, *The Wilderness of God*, p. 67.

[5] Louth, p. 68.

[6] Montaldo, p. 468.

[7] Louth, p. 68.

[8] Merton, *The Wisdom of the Desert*, p. 55.

[9] Ward, *The Wisdom of the Desert Fathers*, p. 39.
[10] Ward, p. 29.

Day Six

Becoming a Saint—*Becoming Yourself*

Coming Together in the Spirit

"I want to know God's thoughts... The rest are details." These are not the words of one of the world's foremost theologians but one of the world's foremost scientists—Dr. Albert Einstein.

On this retreat day we will be looking at "God's thoughts" about you and me—and how God wants each of us to become a saint, which was the life focus of every Desert Mystic. Like Einstein, these early men and women ascetics were trying to discern God's thoughts, not the world's or even their own. Neither were they seeking to become saints for their own sake—but for God's. Like Mother Teresa of Calcutta, they wanted to not only *do* something beautiful for God, they wanted to *be* something beautiful for God.

For the Desert Christian this meant not being deterred by life's many hardships, large and small; rather, they welcomed these hardships and tried to keep a "God's eye perspective" on things. They devoted their minds and hearts to compliance with God's thoughts and God's will. This was the path that they followed in the desert—the path to personal holiness and to eternal life.

And just what did these saintly men and women conclude God's thoughts to be? That we, each of us, become the persons we were meant to be. "When you die and go to heaven," reminds Jewish writer Elie Wiesel, "our maker is not going to ask, 'why didn't you discover the cure for such and such? Why didn't you become the Messiah?' The only question we will be asked in that precious moment is, 'why didn't you become you?'"

So it is that we, too, walk in the footsteps of these *ordinary, human folks* who were called into the desert to follow Christ. Ordinary? Human? While this may seem to be a paradox, it is very important. Writes Thomas Merton of the Desert Mystics in his *The Wisdom of the Desert*:

> If we reflect a moment, we will see that to fly to the desert in order to be extraordinary is only to carry the world with you as an implicit standard of comparison. The result would be nothing but self-contemplation, and self-comparison with the negative standard of the world one had abandoned. Some of the monks of the Desert did this, as a matter of fact: and the only fruit of their trouble was that they went out of their heads. The simple men who lived their lives out to a good old age among the rocks and sands only did so because they had come into the desert to be themselves, their *ordinary* selves, and to forget a world that divided them from themselves. There can be no other valid reason for seeking solitude or for leaving the world. And thus to leave the world, is, in fact, to help it in saving oneself... Then they had not only the power but even the obligation to pull the whole world to safety after them.[1]

Defining Our Thematic Context

Writer Edward Abbey, of *Desert Solitaire* fame, and one of the earliest of modern environmentalists, used to like telling the following story: There are always tourists coming to visit me in the desert, and they always ask the same thing: "Does it ever rain here?" And I always respond: "I don't know; I've only been here 28 years."[2]

How long have you been "where you are"? Has life rained on you? Has life's rain—and sunshine—changed you? That's what this retreat session is all about: change.

Indeed, in every life (and even in every desert!) "a little rain must fall." And rain has the power to change things. But we have the power within ourselves to change things also—even ourselves, when we open ourselves up to God's graces.

"For me to be a saint," writes Thomas Merton in *New Seeds of Contemplation*, "means to be myself. Therefore the problem of sanctity and salvation is in fact the problem of finding out who I am and discovering my true self."[3]

He continues:

> Trees and animals have no problem. God makes them what they are without consulting them, and they are perfectly satisfied. With us it is different. God leaves us free to be whatever we like. We can be ourselves or not, as we please... Therefore there is only one problem in which all my existence, my peace and my happiness depend: to discover myself in discovering God. If I find Him I will find myself and if I find my true self I will find Him.[4]

Opening Prayer

Dear God,
Shower me with
A good cleansing rain,
A rain to wash away the
Layers upon layers of disguises I wear,

So that when the rain stops
I may look into a reflecting pool
And see only the one
You want me to see there.
Amen.

Retreat Session Six

Are you a "double"? I'm a double. I'm almost always "of two minds." I learned recently that almost all the words that start with "dis" have a pejorative sense to them. And it's primarily because they always refer to the doubt and dissolution and disorientation that our "duality" or "split" or double-focus can bring!

If we are human—and most of us are—we are going to have to come to terms with this duality, this "two-mindedness." I like the way Saint James cuts to the chase and addresses this human weakness we all possess:

> If any of you is lacking in wisdom, ask God, who gives to all generously and ungrudgingly, and it will be given you. But ask in faith, not doubting, for the one who doubts is like a wave of the seas, driven and tossed by the wind. For the doubter being double-minded and unstable in every way must not expect to receive anything from the Lord. (James 1:5-8)

Today, as I write this, I am living in "two places": My body is residing here at an "artificial paradise"—a resort hotel where every resident has an oceanfront room. (I'm attending a corporate convention, and the emphasis is on corporate!) So in many ways my mind is back home even though my body is here. I'm as far away as one can get from a desert, and yet it feels like one in many ways. The grass is too green, the landscape too beautiful, the meals too well-planned, the people too polite ("too happy," as my daughter would say). It's all too unreal and superficial. What is particularly interesting as I analyze my "place" in all of this is the following: I have no sense of *belonging*. Nor does it appear that most of the folks here do. While our whole world here is comprised of a magnificent blue ocean and a magnificently plush hotel, everyone is out on the sandy beach! There is a big stretch of sand between me and the ocean as I look out off my hotel-room balcony. And there are the people: not in the water, not in the hotel, but there in the most "desert" place of all—right there on the sandy beach. They're in this sort of "buffer zone," a "no-one's land" that has become everyone's land!

I ask myself and you: Isn't this scene very much like what the Desert Mystics witnessed and experienced in their day, as they searched for a comfort zone, a place of belonging? Let me be more specific:

Much of the Christian life is a struggle to figure out just where we belong. We are constantly, in our minds and hearts, struggling between the attractions of the physical and the spiritual worlds. While some Great Voice inside of us tells us we are all destined for something wonderful and mystical, a land far beyond our wildest imaginations, we also know that we need to keep our feet on the ground (or the sand!) in the meantime. We belong neither securely ensconced in our fancy hotel rooms with room service and in-room first-run movies...nor do we belong just yet out there in the mysterious and deep blue ocean. Instead—we run to the beaches. It's where we belong...for now.

And it's where the Desert Mystics ran to as well.

Yes, they ran to something, and they were *for*

something, as we have emphasized earlier. They went to a place where God was unavoidable, but they didn't totally eliminate themselves or their neighbors in the process. Writer John Howard Griffin, in his book, *The Hermitage Journals: A Diary Kept While Working on the Biography of Thomas Merton*, puts all of this into powerful perspective, as he adds some necessary caution to us modern seekers:

> Men who put away everything that is not God run the risk of putting away everything that is not themselves; of putting away many things that are manifestations of God, and putting away God in the process. It is really not a question of putting away anything, but of allowing oneself to be stripped of whatever God wants. Some religions manage heroically to practice an asceticism that sieves out everything except their prejudices and antipathies, which takes on the robe of militant virtue dedicated to God (quite sincerely), and so they end up in the atrophy of hating for the love of God. In the religious life they have to act...and their actions are almost never for a thing but rather 'anti-' things: anti-communist, anti-renewal, anti-everything that is not in conformity with their prejudices. Their cumulative message seems to be not that men should be like Christ, but that men should be like them who are like Christ. What nonsense.[5]

And now, while we're running off to places where we belong, and while we're speaking in symbols and metaphors, let's go one level deeper:

Where do we truly belong, each and every one of us? *We belong intimately in love with God*. But reaching intimacy, too, has its stages, as every one of us who has ever loved comes to know very well.

Do you remember falling in love—genuinely in love,

when you knew it was love pure and simple and love grand and wondrous and nothing less? Chances are, even though we may say we fell suddenly head over heels in love, or we may even say we went out "looking for love," it most likely came in stages and, for the most part, by accident. The love and the intimacy most likely grew—or "happened"—bit by wonderful bit.

So it is with our love affair with God. Like the Desert Mystics, we may set out for the barren desert looking for a love affair, though it is more likely that we go there just to be available to God. And, as with human love, it begins not with soul-bearing statements to the object of our love, but with small hints and inklings. We don't say immediately, "Don't you see what I'm feeling?" or "Don't you see who I really am?" No. Instead we make small revelations about ourselves—things like, "Oh, I just love Mozart...or Vonnegut...or gardening...or what-have-you." And it grows from there, especially as the other person makes revelations back to us. Intimacy may begin with words, or actions, or tenderness—but it invariably ends up simply with "presence." And that's enough.

And this is the way it is as we strive to follow Jesus' command to love God with all our hearts and minds and souls. It happens, it just happens, when we reveal ourselves, when we make ourselves available and make ourselves known to God. God, in turn, is revealed to us. And, lo and behold, we're in love, whether we know it or not. Someone once said that the best prayer is when you don't even know it's prayer. We might go so far as to even say that the best love is when we don't even know it's love.

I love Thomas Merton's down-to-earth sentiment about love of God, articulated in his early journals and written before his entry into the monastic life: "It is terrible to want to belong entirely to God, and see nothing around you but the world, and not see Him. In the monastery you don't see Him either, but you have nothing to do but lament your separation from Him, and to pray to Him, and pray for the world."[6] We do the same in our own monasteries and deserts and beaches.

And let us conclude this section with a Merton sentiment, as well. For indeed, he possessed an incomparable grasp of what mystics, as well as ordinary folks simply trying to please God, must try to achieve:

> We cannot do exactly what they [the Desert Mystics] did. But we must be as thorough and as ruthless in our determination to break all spiritual chains, and cast off the domination of alien compulsions, to find our true selves, to discover and develop our inalienable spiritual liberty and use it to build, on earth, the Kingdom of God. This is not the place in which to speculate what our great and mysterious vocation might involve. That is still unknown. Let it suffice for me to say that we need to learn from these men of the fourth century how to ignore prejudice, defy compulsion and strike out fearlessly into the unknown.[7]

It has been said that the reason people don't build cathedrals anymore is that people used to have convictions; now they have opinions. The Desert Mystics had convictions; and they built cathedrals. But the cathedrals they built are the same ones we can build: little "shanties" that glorify God because they have been built with great sincerity, with great genuineness, with great conviction.

Let us close with this provocative tale from the sayings, which emphasizes we are not asked, any of us, to impose totally alien practices or personas upon ourselves to be pleasing to God. *It may be the most important of all the sayings, when we get right down to it!*

A brother asked an old man: "What thing is so good that I may do it and live by it?" And the old man said: "God alone knows what is good. Yet I have heard that one of the Fathers asked the great Abba Nesteros, who was a friend of Abba Anthony and said to him: 'what good work shall I do?' And Anthony replied 'Cannot all works please God equally? Scripture says, "Abraham was hospitable and God was with him. And Elijah loved quiet, and God was with him. And David was humble and God was with him. So whatever you find your soul wills in following God's will, do it, and keep your heart."'"[8]

For Reflection

- *What is the sound—and the volume of the sound at this time in your life—of God's call to you?*
- *When have you put yourself "out there"...out where you were entirely dependent on God?*

Closing Prayer

Lord, I want to pitch my tent out there in the desert with you.
And I want to drive the anchor-stakes in deep,
Because I know the stakes are high!
Help me to weather all the storms of doubt and fear as they
Come along, as they most certainly will.
I know that my own personal "desert" may be such things as sickness,
Weariness, spiritual dryness, my job, the people I live with
The people who live with me—

and even my own approaching death
And its accompanying tribulations.
Help me, during the most parched and forlorn
of times
To pray this "desert prayer" along with the
prophet Isaiah:
The wilderness and the dry land
Shall be glad,
The desert shall rejoice and blossom...abundantly
Then the eyes of the blind shall be opened,
And the ears of the deaf unstopped;
Then the lame shall leap like a deer,
And the tongue of the speechless sing for joy.
For waters shall break forth in the wilderness,
And streams in the desert...
And the ransomed of the Lord shall return,
And come to Zion with singing;
Everlasting joy shall be upon their heads;
They shall obtain joy and gladness,
And sorrow and sighing shall flee away.
(Isaiah 35: 1-2, 5-6, 10)

Notes

[1] Merton, *The Wisdom of the Desert*, pp. 22-23.

[2] Edward Abbey, *Confessions of a Barbarian*, p. 133.

[3] Merton, *New Seeds of Contemplation*, p. 31.

[4] Merton, p. 36.

[5] John Howard Griffin, *The Hermitage Journals: A Diary Kept While Working on the Biography of Thomas Merton* (Garden City, N.Y.: Image Books, 1983), p. 101.

[6] Hart, *Run to the Mountain: The Journals of Thomas Merton*, p. 357.

[7] Merton, *The Wisdom of the Desert*, p. 23.

[8] Squire, *Asking the Fathers*, p. 110.

Day Seven

Recognizing the Oasis When We See It—*Blooming Where We Are Planted*

Coming Together in the Spirit

Jesuit priest and poet Gerard Manley Hopkins once wrote, "What you look at hard seems to look at you." Knowing just how mystical Hopkins could be, I'm sure he was ultimately referring to God. But I think he may very well have also been referring to all of creation and our place in it. On this day of our retreat we are going to examine the idea of place, the idea of sacred space—and what we do and who we are when we *look* at our place and space as sacred. Like the Desert Mystics, we shall try to come to a full appreciation and respect for the holy ground we stand on—even if the ground sometimes seems more like a sandy marsh!

Nature writer Annie Dillard, in *For the Time Being*, has written whole sections on something so seemingly insignificant as sand. Why sand? Because it matters. "There is a rough progression in the [Dillard's] book from material and temporal to spiritual and eternal," writes Michael Farrell in his review of her new book:

> And why not sand? She explains its place in the scheme of things. Part of earth, where she lives, as we do, sand matters. The more spherical a grain of

> sand, the older it likely is, she writes. She quotes an expert to the effect that an average river requires a million years to move a grain of sand a hundred miles. Dillard doesn't ask if anyone cares. She writes out of the conviction that it matters, that it's an integral part of our roller-coaster ride. Sooner or later each grain of sand spends time in a desert, just as every American sooner or later visits Disneyland. "Most of the round sand grains in the world, wherever you find them, have spent part of their histories blowing around a desert."[1]

So what's the point of all this? Interconnectedness. Yes, the sand we see in our child's sandbox may have actually been in the desert at some time or another. But, bigger than that, it is not unlikely that we are all Desert folks. And, bigger still than that, as some great poet (or was it a scientist?) put it: We are all stardust!

The danger, then, for all of us on a spiritual quest, is to say to ourselves: Well, easy for the Desert Monk to become a Mystic; he didn't have to contend with our greedy American culture. Or: Easy for Antony to become a saint; he lived in blissful isolation and didn't have all the worldly distractions we have.

Well, none of these excuses "hold water" for the serious Christ-follower. It's just that some of us may have to look at something (or Someone) a little "harder" before we discover it is clearly looking back at us.

Defining Our Thematic Context

For the Desert Mystics, the desert was "a place apart." It is easy for all of us to say something like: Well, give me an airplane ticket to a desert resort and I'll get holy there, too! All of this "desert spirituality" is nothing but a romantic illusion. Get real! We live in the real world!

Well, a place apart is getting to be more and more of an illusion in our modern world where places of wilderness and retreat are few and far between. Just this morning I took a walk as I am here on retreat at the Abbey of Gethsemani. I walked about two miles from the monastery out onto a road that I thought was pretty secluded. Lo and behold, what do I find? Not less than six fellow retreatants, one at a time, coming and going, do I encounter on my "private" walk! One of the retreatants even mutters to me in a friendly way: "Sure is a popular place." "Sure is!" I reply. It made me think of how the earliest natives of Las Vegas must have felt. There they were (very few of them!) in the middle of the desert. And now: a veritable metropolis full of commerce and entertainment. As a matter of fact, I saw recently that Las Vegas is the meeting place of many modern conventioneers—and most notably the site for the National Funeral Directors Convention! Their meeting hours? Noon until three p.m. only! The rest of the time it's death- (and desert-) *denial*!

But can you blame them? And can you blame us for wanting to deny death? After all, it is resurrection that Jesus came to promise and deliver—not death.

Perhaps a greater problem today than denying death is feeding our lives...too much. We seem to "have to have" everything in our consumer society. We have to have the latest and the best and the most. This is the mentality the Desert Mystics went away from in order to renounce. We can do the same, in lots of little ways.

And speaking more about "getting away from," it's important to remember that the Desert Mystics were not all solitaries, or hermits. The world wouldn't let them be, in many cases. Just as Saint Benedict a century or so later kept getting "sought out" and "sought after" until he established a monastic community, many of the

Desert Mystics encountered the same experience. As Christianity became "legalized"—after years and years of persecution—it soon became haute, and the Desert Fathers and Mothers found themselves overrun by crowds from Rome and Alexandria. It is said, in fact, that the desert population came to actually equal that of the towns! (This is something of what we are experiencing at monastery retreat houses these days—not to mention on our retreatant prayer-walks, far out into the hills on the monastery grounds.) Well, a "convention" of Christians can't be a bad thing, no matter where!

Opening Prayer

O God, you are my God, I seek you,
  my soul thirsts for you;
my flesh faints for you,
  as in a dry and weary land where there is no water.
So I have looked upon you in the sanctuary,
  beholding your power and glory. (Psalm 62:1-2)

RETREAT SESSION SEVEN

Instead of calling this chapter or retreat day, "Recognizing the Oasis When We See It: Blooming Where You Are Planted," I was tempted to call it something along the lines of a continuation of the last chapter...something like: "The Grandest Vocation: Becoming Yourself"

But enough about you—for right now. May I tell you about *me*? If so, let me begin by saying that my heroes have always been mystics. I believe we need heroes more than ever today, and it is a good practice to keep asking ourselves just who our heroes are. Do we want to "Be Like Mike"...or Pachomius...Thomas Merton...or some totally unheralded individual who simply tries to do what is right and walk humbly with God? Who do we want to grow up and be like?

I have just returned from a prayer-walk here on retreat at the Abbey of Gethsemani. And what did I, a 51-year-old married man and the father of three children, ponder and pray about out there on my prayer-walk? *My vocation*, for heaven's sake! "What do I want to be when I grow up?"

It's a necessary question, I think, no matter what our age and "position." But...to continue my "true confessions" in order to make a point:

Let me say that much of who I am revolves around the work I do. I am the publisher at Abbey Press, a Benedictine-owned firm in Saint Meinrad, Indiana, not terribly far from the farm I grew up on. And Saint Meinrad is also the place where I attended seminary as a young boy/man, for five years in the 1960's, trying to see if I had a vocation to the Catholic priesthood. In 1966 I decided that I did not, that perhaps it was a teacher, a college professor, a journalism or writing career that I was more suited for.

So I left the counter-cultural world of the seminary (a desert, really) in 1966 and entered another counter-culture: the world of a state university. There I was never happier, wilder, freer—and, quite often, miserable. Depressed is another good word for it. Why depressed? I was absolutely *lost* spiritually. I had discarded absolutely everything I had previously believed about God and religion as irrelevant. I'll have another Budweiser instead of God, thank you. Oh, and pass me the Thomas Wolfe, the Hemingway, the Salinger, the Janis Joplin and the

John Berryman. These are the guys who really know where it's at. (Three out of five of them killed themselves, but that was a big part of what made them cool. I was killing myself anyway, deadening every sensibility I had. And my soul was already dead. Or so I thought.)

In the late 1960's I re-met God. She was Irish, and her name was Michaelene O'Neal. Well, she wasn't really God, but she was the kindest and most loving person I had ever met and have still ever met. Reader, I married her.

In 1974 we wed, and by then I was an "associate" editor at Abbey Press, loving my wife and my work both so much that I never wanted to leave them. In them both I rediscovered God. In my wife I saw the love of God manifested like never before; in my work as a Catholic editor I was "forced" to read religious and spiritual literature that I would never have picked up on my own. And do you know what happens after you start reading a lot of stuff? You start believing it! For me, it was re-believing it.

It was that same year that I was invited to come to Cincinnati to work for *St. Anthony Messenger*, the premiere Catholic magazine of its time, and the premiere one still today, in my view. It was published by the Franciscans, and they were a joy to work for and taught me a lot about poverty of the spirit (but they paid me well!). So wife "Mikie" and I moved to Cincinnati, struck out on our own, to face a new and exciting life and to start a family.

Well, the family didn't come...and didn't come. We went through three painful miscarriages over the years, each one more difficult than the last. But we did, happily, put in for adoption, and after a three-year wait were given baby Michael. Joy of joys! He's now a student at Purdue University and is not only brilliant; he's truly a nice guy to be around.

Then in 1982 we had baby Emily—yes, a pregnancy taken to full term, and full fruit! Emily now graces us with her presence (whenever she feels like it!) as an 18-year-old. Pretty, smart, gifted, funny, wonderful... May I go on?

In 1987 baby Patrick came along. He's now a gangly 14-year-old and is God-like (like his mother) and weird, sorta, (like his father). He will go far, as soon as he figures out where to go. We hope that's not soon.

Intermingled with all these births have been deaths, as every family experiences sooner or later. In addition to our loss through miscarriage, we have lost all four of our parents, and some very good friends, as well. And we've seen a lot of suffering. And, a lot of...*change*.

In 1987 I changed jobs, coming back to Indiana and Abbey Press to start up a publishing program called One Caring Place. Our main publication line: *CareNotes*. This was to be not just a job; this was to be my vocation. And it has been. Said one wise writer: "The only vocation any of us can really have in life is to help ease the suffering in the world." I believe that. And the Caring publication program has been a phenomenal success, if I may say so myself. We've circulated well over fifty million of the little *CareNotes* now and the name has become pretty much a household word in so many churches and hospitals and caring places. This is surely God's work, and I am today involved in it as much as ever. It is reassuring to me in some ways that one of the sayings of the Desert Mystics addresses this idea of supporting and comforting those who suffer:

A brother said to an old man, "There are two brothers. One of them stays in his cell quietly, fasting for six days at a time, and imposing on himself a good deal of discipline, and the other serves the sick. Which one of them is more acceptable to God?" The old man replied,

"Even if the brother who fasts six days were to hang himself by the nose, he could not equal the one who serves the sick."[2]

No, I don't dare compare myself to the brother who serves the sick. Sometimes I think my good intentions boil down to a credo that falls pretty short, and goes something like this: "I believe that lepers should be hugged. May I encourage you to hug one? I'll stay here and publish books all about it."

But what about this *other* thing...this search for the *spiritual*—for my own life, and to encourage it in others? This is why I write books like this, of course! It's also the reason in 1994 I wrote a little book called, *Prayer-Walking*. I'm proud (but also somewhat embarrassed) to say this book was featured in *USA Today* and *The Washington Post* and has been on TV and radio stations and in a score of magazines throughout the country. Many thousands of copies of the book have been sold and I have given numerous workshops and presentations on walking meditation.

And what has all of this taught me? That there is power, and there can be God's power, in words—the right words: healing words, inspiring words. But it has also taught me to be wary of my demons—just as every good Desert Mystic needed to be.

Just who and what are these demons?

- The demon that says it is me that is doing all this good—and not God using me as an instrument of Divine love.
- The demon that won't let us admit that greatness is overrated, but instead that achievement, accomplishment, efficiency, sales, success are the things that matter—and that "Being still and knowing that I am God" is a line out of a fairy tale.

- The demon that keeps telling me I have to "do something worthwhile" to earn God's love—but doesn't let me translate the word worthwhile as preparing myself to accept God's love.
- The demon that tells me I know what is best for me—and that God surely wants what I want.
- The demon that tells me that I have to save the world—and that Jesus didn't do it well enough.
- The demon who tells me I am a master, a teacher, a prophet, a genius—and doesn't remind me I don't even tie my shoes all that well.
- The demon that says freedom is everything—and scorns anyone who cries, "If this be freedom, lock me up in your arms, O Lord!"
- The demon that suggests you say to the Lord and yourself: "If only I had more time."
- The demon that tells me I have bigger fish to fry than others do—but doesn't bother to tell me that I become the demon's "fish," caught hook, line and sinker, when I buy this thinking.
- The demon that tells me, "Sure, you're a husband, but what about all those people out there who need you?"
- The demon that tells me, "Sure, you're a father, but what about writing another article on the spiritual life this weekend instead of spending time with your daughter who will be gone from your household in two years?"
- The demon that says, "If you write just one more chapter; read just one more book; make just one more retreat; recite just one more prayer...and all will be

well"—but doesn't tell us "the rest of the story": None of this is really in our hands!

- The demon that tells me that the Desert Mystics were "Pre-Vatican II, for heaven's sake"—but fails to also remind me that so was Jesus.
- The demon that says you have nothing to fear on judgment day—after all, just look at all you've done.
- The demon that says: "Emptiness Shmemptiness! Go and get your fill of life!"—and doesn't dare let us think that God can only enter a place where there is room.

Thomas Merton wrote in his journal on March 11, 1948: "Before dinner I was brooding about it and thinking: 'The people in the world are so eager to hear about contemplation and monks hate it. What is the matter?'"[3]

Why is it that "the grass is always greener"? I remember the first time I came to the Trappist monastery at Gethsemani for a retreat. I had the privilege of meeting monk Matthew Kelty. And one of the first things he told me was there were a lot of people out in the world who were "monk happy." His point was: If only us *monks* were so "monk happy"; well, many of them are.

They are happy because they are "blooming where they are planted." They are putting into practice that famous old saying about first acquiring *interior peace...* "and a whole host of people will find their salvation in you."

And we can do the same. Contemplation, conversion, holiness...these are not a matter of place, even if place is important. "We simply have to be where we are with a different state of mind," says Joan Chittister, O.S.B.[4] What the Desert Mystics wanted, and what all mystics and today's folks with monk-hearts and mystic-hearts want, is conversion. But conversion to what? "The answer never changes," says Chittister. "To be contemplative we must be in tune with the Sound of the universe. We must become aware of the sacred in every single element of life. We must bring beauty to birth in a poor and plastic world. We must heal the human community...[It is] about becoming more contemplative all the time. It is about being in the world differently."[5]

Let's close out this session on "blooming where you are planted," with an appropriate Desert Saying, followed with a very powerful piece of "leavening" wisdom entitled "A Much-Needed Letter on Moderation," and ascribed to the mystical author of *The Cloud of Unknowing*. First, from the Desert:

An old man was asked: "What is necessary to do to be saved?" He was making rope, and without looking up from the work, he replied, "You are looking at it."[6]

And from *The Cloud of Unknowing*, this beautiful summary to help us balance all of this:

> Put the strict way on one side and the lax way on the other, and look instead for what is hidden between them; once you have found this you will be free in spirit to pick up or leave any of the other things as you wish...What, you may ask, is this hidden something? Quite simply it is God...God is hidden between them and you cannot find him with your intelligence...So choose him, and you will be silently speaking, speaking silence, eating in fasting, fasting in eating, and so forth... This loving choice of God, knowing what to set aside in order to seek him out with the steadfastness of a pure heart, being able to put both opposites aside when they present themselves as the be-all and end-all of spiritual aspirations, the best way of finding God you can learn in this life.[7]

For Reflection

- *How content are you to stay in the wilderness of chaos and confusion and "on-the-way-ness"?*
- *How do you cope with the emptiness in your own private desert? Do you have to fill it up...with noise, with things, even with "good things"—good things like flowing water, the score of last night's ballgame, a drink when you get home, the latest book (even if it's Stephen King's or John Irving's or the Pope's?) or the latest computer game?*
- *"The will of God will not take you where the grace of God cannot keep you." To what good destination is God taking you in your spiritual journey? Are you trusting God to keep you there?*

Closing Prayer

"Lord, I am happy that
I can at least
want to love You."
Amen.
—*Thomas Merton*[8]

Notes

[1] Michael Farrell, "Annie Dillard Demands That We Look Life in the Eye," *National Catholic Reporter*, May 7, 1999, p. 31.

[2] Mayers, *Listen to the Desert*, p. 121.

[3] Montaldo, *Entering the Silence*, p. 181.

[4] Chittister, "Millennial Wisdom Stirs in the Desert," p. 36.

[5] Chittister, p. 36.

[6] Mayers, p. 105.

[7] Mayers, p. 113.

[8] Montaldo, p. 174.

Going Forth to Live the Theme

For the serious Christian, times haven't changed much, really. Much of the modern Christian's life still centers around the idea and question of *purpose*. And so we ask ourselves again and again, just as the Desert Mystics did: "Why did God put me here?" And then, further: "Am I here to *do* or to *be*?" "Am I here to be *active* or to be *contemplative*? The answer, invariably, ends up to be: both. And that's true whether one is a Chief Executive Officer (CEO) or a Manifestation of the Nonperishable Kingdom (MONK).

Trappist monk Matthew Kelty doesn't mind admitting that monks are pretty "useless"—or at least they appear to be—not unlike a work of art. And, not unlike a work of art, there is "exaggeration" present, in order to make a point. Someone once asked a monk friend of mine: "Nice. But what do monks really DO?" And the monk replied, "Well, nothing really, except work and pray." To which the questioner whimsically responded, "Well, I guess that's pretty impressive when you get enough of them doing it!"

But what do monks do for the world? What did the "quiet, inactive" Desert Mystics do for the world? What do we would-be contemplatives really *do* for the world? Writer Martin Marty, in his newsletter, *Context*, quotes C. S. Lewis on this profound question:

> If you read history you will find that Christians who did the most for the present world were just those who thought most of the next. The apostles

> themselves, who set on foot the conversion of the Roman Empire, the great men who built up the Middle Ages, the English evangelicals who abolished the slave trade, all left their mark on earth precisely because their minds were occupied with heaven. It is since Christians have largely ceased to think of the other world that they have become so ineffective in this one. Aim at heaven and you will get earth "thrown in." Aim at earth and you will get neither.[1]

In much of Thomas Merton's writings, we read this same theology and philosophy. Merton chimed in with this age-old belief that monks were to be depended upon for prayers for the sake of the world; they were to be the defenders of the faith, and through them the world was kept in being and human life preserved and honored by God. Monks are seen as the guardians of the world's peace, constantly keeping their eye on the frontiers lest the attackers approach, laboring and praying to keep the demons at bay—not only protecting themselves from the demons but the entire world. Not only praying for their own salvation, the Desert Mystics were seen as "workers" for the world's salvation.

One specific example of this may serve as a symbol of this "guardianship": There is the story of Antony of the Desert who planted vegetables in order to have food for himself and his visitors. But first he had to ward off the beasts who trampled his crops as they came to his garden for water. "But gently capturing one of the beasts, he said to all of them, 'Why do you hurt me, when I do you no injury? Leave, and in the name of the Lord do not come near here any longer.' From then on, as if being afraid of the command, they did not come near the place."[2] In the Middle Ages society as a whole came to be separated into three segments: those who fight, those who labor, and those who pray. And the chief prayers, the monks—those who chanted the psalms and prayed constantly—were seen as not unlike trees which purify the atmosphere by their very presence.

From my own experience I can say with great conviction that, yes, it has been the go-getters who have inspired me, but it has been the quiet, inactive, "eyes-on-the-prize" people who have made me whole and "purified" me (to some limited degree!) by their very presence: people like Elaine Knapp, O.S.B., Camillus Ellsperman, O.S.B., Matthew Kelty, OCSO, Joseph Mundy, Betty Hopf, S.P., Dave Stipp, Michaelene O'Neal… Desert Mystics, one and all!

Let me close, simply, with The Ten Commandments (For Would-Be Desert Mystics—Like You and Me):

I. Thou shalt have no other God than God, and shall not make a God of thine own holiness or thy desert search for it.

II. Thou shalt recognize that thou art a sinner and that thou shalt take the heat for it thyself.

III. Thou shalt know that silence is golden.

IV. Thou shalt recognize the greatest sin is the sin of indifference or complacency—and not the sins of sex or greed or theft, even though these latter sins shall also be avoided.

V. Thou shalt know the seed must die or else it cannot bring forth life from itself.

VI. Thou shalt not covet thy neighbor's oasis, but recognize thine own oasis when thou seeth it, blooming where thou art planted—or where God desireth to plant thee.

VII. Thou shalt call a mirage a mirage.

VIII. Thou shalt keep always on the lookout for shade: the cool shade that only God can provide.

IX. Thou shalt thank God for palm trees and springs of living water.

X. Thou shalt pray always for rain…the reign of God.

Notes

[1] Martin Marty, *Context*, May 15, 1999.

[2] Robert C. Gregg, *Athanasius: The Life of Antony and the Letter to Marcellinus* (Mahwah, N.J.: Paulist Press, 1980), p. 69.

Deepening Your Acquaintance

Sanctitate et Scientia: Holiness...and the Love of Learning: In addition to this being the motto of the Saint Meinrad School of Theology, with which I am happy to be associated, Holiness and Learning are ancient Christian aspirations. Holiness, after all, is what we Christians are seeking, and Learning and the Love of it can help us along the journey.

The following books are intended to help retreatants sustain their relationship with the Desert Mystics, but in a larger sense to help the Christian seeker of Holiness and the Love of Learning. May they be sources for you of spiritual knowledge and inspiration.

Driscoll, Jeremy, ed. *The Mind's Long Journey to the Holy Trinity: The Ad Monachos of Evagrius Ponticus.* Collegeville, Minn.: The Liturgical Press, 1993.

Funk, Margaret Mary. *Thoughts Matter: The Practice of the Spiritual Life.* New York: Continuum, 1998.

Gregg, Robert C. *Athanasius: The Life of Antony and the Letter to Marcellinus.* Mahwah, N.J.: Paulist Press, 1980.

Housden, Roger. *Retreat: Time Apart for Silence and Solitude.* San Francisco, Calif.: HarperCollins, 1995.

Lawrence, C. H. *Medieval Monasticism: Forms of Religious Life in Western Europe in the Middle Ages.* Essex, England: Longman Group UK Limited, 1984.

Louth, Andrew. *The Wilderness of God.* Nashville, Tenn.: Abingdon Press, 1991.

Lubheid, Colm. *John Cassian Conferences*. Mahwah, N.J.: Paulist Press, 1968.

Merton, Thomas. *New Seeds of Contemplation*. New York: New Directions, 1961.

_____. *The Wisdom of the Desert*. New York: New Directions, 1960

_____. *Woods, Shore, Desert*. Santa Fe, N.M.: Museum of New Mexico Press, 1982

Montaldo, Jonathan, ed. *Entering the Silence: The Journals of Thomas Merton*, Volume II 1941-1952. San Francisco: HarperCollins, 1996.

Mundy, Linus. *A Retreat With Benedict and Bernard: Seeking God—Alone and Together.* Cincinnati, Ohio: Saint Anthony Messenger Press, 1998.

____.*The Complete Guide to Prayer-Walking*. New York: The Crossroad Publishing Company, 1996.

____. *Keep-life-simple Therapy*. Saint Meinrad, Ind.: Abbey Press, 1993.

____. *Slow-down Therapy*. Saint Meinrad, Ind.: Abbey Press, 1991.

Waddell, Helen. *The Desert Fathers*. New York: Vintage Books, 1998.

Ward, Benedicta. *The Wisdom of the Desert Fathers*. Spencer, Mass.: Cistercian Publications, 1986.